Contents

ANNA HAZARE

The Face of India's Fight Against Corruption

ANNA HAZARE

The Face of India's Fight Against Corruption

Editors

Pradeep Thakur

and

Pooja Rana

PENTAGON PRESS

Anna Hazare: The Face of India's Fight Against Corruption
Pradeep Thakur and Pooja Rana (*Eds*)

ISBN 978-81-8274-545-2

First Published in 2011

Published by

PENTAGON PRESS
206, Peacock Lane, Shahpur Jat, New Delhi-110049
Phones: 011-64706243, 26491568
Telefax: 011-26490600
email: rajan@pentagonpress.in
website: www.pentagonpress.in

Printed at Chaman Offset Printers, New Delhi.

Preface

He calls himself a "fakir" a man who has no family, no property and no bank balance. He lives in a small room attached to the Yadavbaba temple in Ahmednagar's Ralegan Siddhi village, 110 km from Pune and wears only khadi. But when 71-year-old **Kisan Baburao Hazare** alias Anna Hazare starts an agitation, every leader from Mumbai to Delhi sits up and takes notice. Even his detractors and politicians, who hate his guts, grudgingly accept he is the only person who has the power to mobilize common people across the country and shake up a government. His small frail body has taken several blows from the countless agitations, tours and hunger strikes he has undertaken since he came in public life in 1975. He lost his mother Laxmibai in 2002 and has two married sisters one in Mumbai and another in Sangamner who worry every time their "stubborn brother starts an indefinite hunger strike".

He once contemplated suicide and even wrote a two-page essay on why he wanted to end his life. Anna Hazare was not driven to such a pass by circumstances. He wanted to live no more because he was frustrated with life and wanted an answer to the purpose of human existence. The story goes that one day at the New Delhi Railway Station, he chanced upon a book on Swami Vivekananda. Drawn by Vivekananda's photograph, he is quoted as saying that he read the book and found his answer—that the motive of his life lay in service to his fellow humans.

Today, Anna Hazare is the face of India's fight against corruption. He has taken that fight to the corridors of power and challenged the government at the highest level. People, the common man and well-known personalities alike, are supporting him in the hundreds swelling to the thousands.

For Anna Hazare, it is another battle. And he has fought quite a few, including some as a soldier for 15 years in Indian Army. He enlisted after the 1962 Indo-China war when the government exhorted young men to join the Army. In 1978, he took voluntary retirement from the 9th Maratha Battalion and returned home to Ralegaon Siddhi, a village in Maharashtra's drought-prone Ahmadnagar. He was 39 years old. He found farmers back home struggling for survival and their suffering would prompt him to pioneer rainwater conservation that put his little hamlet on the international map as a model village.

The villagers revere him. Anna Hazare's fight against corruption began here. He fought first against corruption that was blocking growth in rural India. His organisation is the Bhrashtachar Virodhi Jan Andolan (People's movement against Corruption) and his tool of protest is hunger strikes. And his prime target is corruption.

His weapon is potent. In 1995-96, he forced the Sena-BJP government in Maharashtra to drop two corrupt Cabinet Ministers. In 2003, he forced the Congress-Nationalist Congress Party (NCP) state government to set up an investigation against four ministers. Maharashtra stalwarts like Sharad Pawar and Bal Thackeray have often called his style of agitation nothing short of "blackmail".

But Anna Hazare has soldiered on relentless, from one battle to another in his war against corruption. He fought from the front to have Right to Information (RTI) implemented. He is now fighting for the implementation of the Jan Lokpal Bill, an anti-corruption bill drafted by leading members of civil society that envisages speedy action in corruption cases against everyone, including ministers and senior bureaucrats.

More than 30 years after Anna Hazare started his crusade, as the 72-year-old observes a hunger strike in Delhi against large-scale corruption at the national level, nothing really has changed except the scale of his battle.

I have compiled and edited this book—*Anna Hazare: The Face of India's Fight Against Corruption*—from different news sources quoted in the relevant texts. I am thankful to all of them. I hope this book will create a window to see the challenges of the corruption in all walks of Indian life and the struggle of civil society eventually led by Anna Hazare.

11 April 2011   PRADEEP THAKUR

CHAPTER 1

Introduction

Social activist Anna Hazare's fast unto death for an anti corruption law has stirred people's imaginations, igniting India's one of the biggest mass protests in recent times.

On 5 April 2011, Anna Hazare initiated a movement for passing a strong anti-corruption Lokpal (ombudsman) bill in the Indian Parliament. As a part of this movement, N. Santosh Hegde, a former justice of the Supreme Court of India and Lokayukta of Karnataka, Prashant Bhushan, a senior lawyer in the Supreme Court along with the members of the India Against Corruption movement drafted an alternate bill, named as the Jan Lokpal Bill (People's Ombudsman Bill) with more stringent provisions and wider power to the Lokpal (Ombudsman). Hazare began a fast unto death from 5 April 2011 at Jantar Mantar in Delhi, to press for the demand to form a joint committee of the representatives of the Government and the civil society to draft a new bill with stronger penal actions and more independence to the Lokpal and Lokayuktas (Ombudsmen in the states), after his demand was rejected by the Prime Minister of India Manmohan Singh. Before commencing his 'fast unto death' he stated, "I will fast until Jan Lokpal Bill is passed".

The movement attracted attention very quickly through various media. It has been reported that thousands of people joined to support Hazare's effort. Almost 150 people reportedly joined Hazare in his fast. He said that he would not allow any politician to sit with him in this movement. Politicians like Uma Bharti and Om Prakash Chautala were shooed away by protesters when they came to visit the site where the protest was taking place. A number of social activists including Medha Patkar, Arvind Kejriwal and former IPS officer Kiran Bedi, Jayaprakash Narayan of the Lok Satta have lent their support to Hazare's hunger strike and anti-corruption campaign.

Bollywood came out completely in support of the protests—with famed actors, musicians and directors speaking in support of the movement and Anna Hazare. Director Farah Khan, actor Anupam Kher, music director Vishal, poet-filmmaker Pritish Nandy and actor Tom Alter all visited Jantar Mantar. Meanwhile famed Indian actors Aamir Khan, Hrithik Roshan and Amitabh Bachchan all stated their support for the movement via social networking websites or the media. Oscar winning Indian composer A.R. Rahman also declared his support for the anti-graft movement. Kareena Kapoor, Shabana Azmi, Shekhar Kapur, Sushmita Sen, Bipasha Basu, Shahid Kapoor, Riteish Deshmukh, Vivek Oberoi, Neha Dhupia, Jackky Bhagnani, Shirish Kunder, Kailash Kher, Punit Malhotra all tweeted their support for Anna Hazare further feulling the masses to join the movement. Famed Indo-Qatari artist M.F. Hussain showed his support by drawing a cartoon of Anna Hazare. Indian students at Cambridge University, the former alma-mater of the Indian prime minister also addressed their support for the movement.

In addition to spiritual leaders Sri Sri Ravi Shankar, Swami Ramdev, Swami Agnivesh and former Indian cricketer Kapil Dev, many celebrities showed their public support through micro-blogging site Twitter. There have also been protests in Bangalore, Mumbai, Chennai, and Ahmedabad among other cities of India.

Within a day of the beginning of the agitation, more than 30,000 people pledged their support to the Lokpal Bill. Organisers of the India Against Corruption said 30,000 people from Maharashtra expressed their support on their website. With an active Facebook page comprising of over 60,000 fans and a Twitter profile with more than 3300 followers, the "India Against Corruption" movement has already been a big success. The website has 20,000 members in Mumbai alone. Within a few days the Facebook page for India Against Corruption had more than 150,000 likes. [There was heightened political activity on social networking websites like Twitter and Facebook. Various support group pages and events were created on the websites to show support and rally the masses. Once again the similarities between the Arab world and its use of social networking as a potent weapon to shake the foundations of the state were seen.

According to the *Economic Times* (April 9, 2011): "A total 4.4 million tweets from 8, 26,000 unique users across 79 cities in India in just three days! That is just a sample of Indian sentiments online for Anna Hazare and his crusade against corruption. And it's the people aged between 36 and 45 years who are talking about it the most, followed by those aged above 46. IT city Bangalore ranks third among the top seven cities on this impressive list after Mumbai and Delhi—reveals this quick data tracking of 42,000 sources by city-based Vangal Software & Services Private Limited."

As a result of this movement, on 6 April 2011 Sharad Pawar resigned from the group of ministers formed for reviewing the Draft Lokpal Bill 2010. On 8 April 2011, the Government of

India partly accepted an important demand of the movement; that the committee for drafting the Jan Lokpal Bill be headed by a citizen activist. While the government expressed its inability to fulfill this demand citing severe opposition from politicians, it accepted the compromise formula that there be a politician chairman and an activist, non-politician Co-Chairman. It was reported that Pranab Mukherjee will be the Chairman of the draft committee while Shanti Bhushan will be the co-chairman.

Lokpal Bill Movement: Battle Won, War On

The instant of victory came on Saturday (9 April 2011) at 10.30 A.M. Having humbled a government and captured the imagination of a nation, the frail 73-year-old Anna Hazare broke his fast by first offering sips of water to women who had fasted with him. He then had a glass of juice. It was offered by five-year-old Soumya Kohli, who had come with her father, Neeraj, to witness the historic moment. The Gandhian leader's marathon ended on the fifth morning of his protest with a large crowd of supporters breaking into loud cheers. Hundreds more poured in at Jantar Mantar, ground zero of the campaign, to ensure civil society's participation in drafting the Lokpal Bill. The massive crowd of supporters that had gathered at Jantar Mantar in New Delhi was euphoric. In seconds, the battlefield for fight against corruption took an entirely different hue with people singing and dancing to celebrate their victory over political anarchy—as Anna put it. Firecrackers were burst and faces smeared with gulal.

Hazare held aloft a copy of the official notification constituting a joint committee and said: "In this fight against corruption, India has won, not Anna. You have shown we are united. But the fight must continue... I will not let this public movement die down. If the government does not pass the bill in Lok Sabha in the monsoon session, I will carry the national flag on my shoulders to protest once again... Next on my agenda is working for the right to recall... I know that there will be further impediments in the implementation of this new bill, which will ensure action against corrupt politicians and bureaucrats and bring in accountability"

His question "Will you support me?" had the crowd roaring in affirmation: "*Anna tum sangharsh karo, hum tumhare saath hain.*" Archbishop Vincent M Concessao, Medha Patkar, Swami Agnivesh and Kiran Bedi besides Arvind Kejriwal were present on the occasion. The 73-year-old Gandhian leader, clearly happy with what he had achieved, led the crowd to sing patriotic songs like Ragupati Raghav Raja Ram and Vande Mataram. He had had nothing to eat for four days but the energy and enthusiasm with which he addressed the crowd was exhilarating. More than 10,000 people had gathered at Jantar Mantar to celebrate the victory. In the morning, people started arriving in droves, so much so that when Anna came on stage to finally offer juice bottles to those fasting with him and break his own fast, there was hardly any space. The crowd was unmanageable. Some people organised havans while others danced.

The warning is well taken. It is a declaration of intent as Hazare and thousands who turned out in his support in several cities will know that their struggle for an effective anti-corruption ombudsman might just be the beginning. Hard negotiation and parliamentary approval lie ahead.

There are larger implications of the four-day revolution. The swiftness with which the official Goliath succumbed to Hazare's simple but powerful message changed some rules the political class feels are immutable. Arrogance of power met an irresistible force. With the grammar of politics and governance rewritten, aftereffects of the civil society getting its foot through the policy door will emerge. Law ministry helped break notification logjam. The deadlock between the government and civil society activists over a notification on a joint committee to draft the Lokpal Bill was broken with law ministry advising Prime Minister Manmohan Singh that such a course of action is feasible. In a letter to the PM on Friday, law minister Veerappa Moily said that while there is no precedent for a government order for a joint committee at the Centre, this can be considered.

Grand finale was at India Gate: After a four-daylong protest against corruption, it was celebration time. People turned up in large numbers at India Gate on Saturday evening for a candlelight vigil to rejoice over their "first victory" against corruption. They said the fight will continue. At six in the evening, India Gate was bustling with activity. Holding the national flag, people could be seen shouting slogans like "*Yeh hamari jeet hai!*" and asking everyone to participate in the fight against corruption. Holding candles and waving the Tricolour, people sang the National Anthem and patriotic songs. A large number of people had come to meet Anna Hazare and thank him for leading the fight. But they had to return disappointed as Hazare couldn't make it due to poor health. Arvind Kejriwal and Swami Agnivesh, who attended the candlelight vigil, said that the struggle for corruption-free India has just begun.

Muscular Lokpal likely sooner than later: Although the Jantar Mantar rumble will not be easy to replicate as the *aam admi's* extraordinary anger gave the protest its dangerous edge, more civil society offensives are certain. The debate over unelected people—and unelectable as politicians whisper—wielding power will intensify although the heady April feeling is exhilarating. Somehow, the Gandhi topi-clad man from Maharashtra's heartland seems to have pushed back a weary cynicism over official inaction, offering hope that things can change.

Prime Minister Manmohan Singh in a statement saw "an agreement in our mutual resolve to combat corruption. This is a scourge that confronts all of us. The government intends to introduce the Lokpal Bill in Parliament during the monsoon session. The fact that civil society and government joined hands to evolve a consensus to move this historic legislation augurs well for our democracy."

Parliament will test the resolve of the campaigners but at least this much is certain: India is likely to get a muscular Lokpal sooner than later. The bill may be scrutinised by a standing committee and miss a deadline or two. But the people power on display will make parties and leaders wary. The increasing value of good governance will make such models more attractive. If after Bihar, the current round of assembly elections delivers a thumb down to the "corrupt", the message will begin to sink in.

Campaign Great Leveler, Bridged Poor-rich Gap

After prolonged indifference and "*is desh ka kuch nahin ho sakta*" approach, social awareness and a political consciousness held the popular imagination. Incongruous as it appeared, the well-heeled protestors at Gurgaon's Galleria market handing out Anna badges were on the same plane as a frugal Gandhian fasting at Jantar Mantar. Mahatma might be passé, but Anna Hazare's crusade bridged a few worlds to connect with the urban upper crust. Over the last five days, the Capital's hip and happening rubbed shoulders with kurtaclad rustic folks of Rajasthan. The top-of-the-line SUVs and luxury sedans vied for attention alongside down-market tempos at the protest hotspot on Jantar Mantar Road and adjoining areas.

The anti-graft movement has, well and truly, a great leveller. Sample this. A placard made an impassioned plea to Delhi's swish set—"this is the place to be". The turnout had busted one of new-age India's most enduring political myths—middle class doesn't care about politics and polls.

Many made a beeline for the ground zero of anti-graft crusade, articulating their frustration against the "system", taking their tirade beyond periodic posts on social networking sites. They took to the streets in large numbers to send a grim reminder to government that any reluctance to stem the all-pervasive rot could bring it down in a matter of days. The GenNext came out of "throes of consumerism" and their air-conditioned workstations to volunteer hold candle-light vigils and jive to patriotic chartbusters like "*yeh desh hai veer jawanon ka*" every evening.

Electoral Reforms on Anna Radar

After breaking his fast on Saturday morning, Anna Hazare said he never expected such an overwhelming response to his movement. Anna suffered severe dehydration on Saturday and his condition deteriorated even though he took juice and some rice. Doctors attending to him said his blood pressure level had shot up to 190/100 mmhg and he has been advised not to speak much. The Gandhian leader told the people that in the next few months, he will visit different states and hold meetings to garner support on various issues, including electoral reforms.

He said, "Next, I will work for Right To Recall, which would empower people to recall non-performing corporators and heads of gram panchayats." Anna also hinted on the formation of a national organisation to lead the agitation against corruption and other social issues. He claimed that the Electronic Voting Machines (EVMs) are not tamper-proof. "I have written to the government several times about this and the response has been positive. They should either improve upon the present technology or change the system," he said. He was also of the opinion that the election commission should introduce a new clause for voting rights where the voter could opt for 'no choice' if he/she wasn't happy with the candidate. In case majority of the votes are cast for this category, then the election should be cancelled, Anna said, adding: "Let them bribe and spend as much money as possible. If you remain honest to your conscience, they will also fall in line."

For Good Cause, they All Behaved

Several thousand people sardined into a few thousand square meter spaces would normally be a perfect recipe for frayed tempers, pickpockets and misbehaviour. But this was not the case at the Jan Lokpal Bill agitation. Delhi turned out at its best behaviour for the five-day Anna phenomenon. There was enthusiasm minus the rowdiness and shoulder rubbing, without the molestation and misbehaviour that are the hallmarks of any Delhi event, be it the trade fair or the New Year bash. Delhiites notorious for their disregard for orders, responded like clockwork to pleas from the "*amaran anshan* (fast unto death)" stage, sitting down when asked to and waiting patiently at the registration desk, even uttering the "*pehle aap*" rarity on some occasions.

Young pairs of hands from all sides pulled up rheumatic elderly from the ground and participants at candle-lit marches moved away from the stage whenever reminded about the people on hunger strike and how they were in need of fresh air. Those already seated moved aside to accommodate some more people even when there was no space left. Each evening, as the stage turned into a talent show of sorts, the atmosphere was akin to a rock concert—without the drunken brawls. The announcers too constantly reminded the crowd of how important good behaviour was if there is an assembly for such a cause. There were constant pleas that Jantar Mantar should not be littered— something more or less followed till the last day when there was an outburst of joy.

Over to Social Media now as Protesters Head Home

Facebook, Twitter, You Tube, SMS campaign and continuous media coverage ensured success of the crusade against corruption started by Anna Hazare. It was the reason behind the overwhelming participation of youth and the middle class which is otherwise reticent. Talking to the *Times of India*, the mastermind of the crusade, Arvind Kejriwal, said, "To keep the issue alive, we are going to use the social media. We will update our friends on Facebook and those registered through the mobile on each and every development that takes place in our meetings with the other committee members and government representatives. Their views will be considered."

Kejriwal is one of the five members selected by Anna Hazare to re-draft the Lokpal Bill in consultation with the government-appointed ministers. He said the gazette notification is the beginning and final implementation of the bill will not happen without continuous public support and involvement. He said when Hazare decided to go on a fast-unto-death; they never imagined they would get such a huge response. "For the first two days, we had a limited number of volunteers and public support was also increasing. But due to Facebook and the SMS campaign, lakhs of people in different parts of the country and Indians living abroad joined the movement. And the best part of this was that almost everyone had come here to support the cause and not strictly due to his or her association with us or our organisation. Had it been a protest called for by any organisation, I don't think the response would have been equally good. All this helped us," said Kejriwal.

The Key is Non-violence

Anna Hazare's victory in getting the government nod on greater public participation in drafting of the anti-corruption bill has raised hopes for a peaceful solution to the Naxal problem. Interlocutor and social activist Swami Agnivesh urged the Maoists to give up violence and follow Gandhian principles to fight against government apathy. Agnivesh said, "Anna's public movement should serve as an example. If you stop the killing and adopt Gandhian principles to protest, the country will support your cause. You should learn from Annaji." Agnivesh was appointed as an interlocutor between the Maoists and the government about a year ago. He said, "The home minister asked me to act as a messenger and help them in finding a peaceful solution. I have asked the government to stop use of armed force against the insurgency, and today, I urge my Naxal brothers and sisters to leave the armed struggle because killing people does not help anyone. That is one of the reasons behind the lack of public support to the poor, adivasi people who have been denied any development." Agnivesh said he did not support the Maoists in violence and considered it absolutely wrong and condemnable. "You cannot bring about revolution at gunpoint," he said.

Protest Timeline

13 March 2011

- A group of Delhi residents dressed in white shirts and t-shirts took a four-hour drive around the city to drum up campaign against corruption and rally support for the Jan Lokpal Bill.

28 March 2011

- According to the organisers of the protests held globally on that day—"As many as 45 cities in USA, 40 cities in India and 8 other countries globally joined in an anti-corruption movement. Indians across the globe, as far as from Nagpur to New Jersey and Sydney to Seattle shouted in one voice to enact 'Jan Lokpal Bill' and ratify the UN Convention against Corruption."
- Many of the marchers were planning to continue the movement by joining Anna Hazare's fast in Delhi on April 5 for the same cause.

4 April 2011

- Anna Hazare, the anti corruption activist leader announced his fast unto death till Jan Lokpal Bill is enacted.

5 April 2011

- Anna Hazare, initiated his fast unto death at Jantar Mantar in Delhi.
- Around 6,000 Mumbai residents joined Anna Hazare for a one-day fast to support the demand for implementation of the Jan Lokpal Bill.
- In Pune over 6,000 residents joined the campaign.
- The Freedom Park in Bangalore was the cynosure of all eyes on Thursday as Bangaloreans from all walks of life thronged the place to support Anna Hazare.

7 April 2011

- 2 rounds of talks with the government failed.
- Anna Hazare continued on with his fast.
- Sonia Gandhi, the president of the Indian National Congress party and the head of the National Advisory Council appealed to Anna Hazare to end his indefinite fast.

8 April 2011

- Protests spreaded to Mumbai, Kolkata, Hyderabad, Bangalore, Chennai, Patna, Bhopal, Ahmedabad, Ranchi, Pune, Nashik and Kochi.
- Protests were organised at Jammu University in Jammu, Thiruvananthapuram, Guwahati and Jaipur.
- The government continued to squabble with the activists stating that the bill drafting committee will be headed by a government appointed minister and not a civil society member as the protesters demanded to avoid allowing the government to make the bill less powerful.
- The Prime Minister Dr. Manmohan Singh met with the President of India to outline to her how the government was going ahead with the demands of the population.
- 15 supporters of Anna Hazare on fast were hospitalised.
- Bollywood came out completely in support of the protests—with famed actors, musicians and directors speaking in support of the movement and Anna Hazare. Director Farah Khan, actor Anupam Kher, music director Vishal Dadlani, poet-filmmaker Pritish Nandy and actor Tom Alter all visited Jantar Mantar. Meanwhile famed Indian actors Aamir Khan, Hrithik Roshan and Amitabh Bachchan all stated their support for the movement via social networking websites or the media. Oscar winning Indian composer A. R. Rahman also declared his support for the anti-graft movement. Kareena Kapoor, Shabana Azmi, Shekhar Kapur, Sushmita Sen, Bipasha Basu, Shahid Kapoor, Riteish Deshmukh, Vivek Oberoi, Neha Dhupia, Jackky Bhagnani, Shirish Kunder, Kailash Kher, Punit Malhotra all tweeted their support for Anna Hazare further feulling the masses to join the movement.

- Famed Qatari artist M.F. Hussain showed his support by drawing a cartoon of Anna Hazare.

- Indian students at Cambridge University, the former almamater of the Indian prime minister also addressed their support for the movement.

- Many prominent people from the government agencies as well as from various corporate houses came out in support of the movement. Some of them were—Delhi Metro chief E. Sreedharan, Punj Lloyd chairman Atul Punj, Maruti Suzuki chairman R.C. Bhargava, Hero group's Sunil Munjal, Tata Steel vice-chairman B. Muthuraman, Bajaj Auto Chairman Rahul Bajaj, Godrej Group head Adi Godrej, Biocon Chairman and Managing Director Kiran Mazumdar-Shaw and Kotak Mahindra Bank vice-chairman & managing director Uday Kotak. They all declared their support for Anna Hazare and the movement.

- ASSOCHAM President Dilip Modi and FICCI Director General Rajiv Kumar, both came out in support of the movement too.

- The Government of India accepted the compromise formula that there be a politician chairman and an activist, non-politician Co-Chairman. It was reported that Pranab Mukherjee will be the Chairman of the draft committee while Shanti Bhushan will be the co-chairman.

9 April 2011

- After accepting all the demands of Anna Hazare, the Government of India issued an Official Gazette notification saying that the draft of Lokpal Bill would be made and presented in the coming monsoon session of Lok Sabha.

- Victory celebrations were held all over India from Jantar Mantar—the center of the protests to Jammu, Mumbai,

Nagpur, Chennai, Kolkata, Allahabad and even Anna Hazare's village.

- Bollywood lauded the victory of Anna Hazare, once again echoing their support for the movement and the support of the Indian citizenry.

- Protesters and leaders of the movement alike stated that the path to attaining complete passing of the bill is still a difficult one, and the movement has to see more harsher days ahead.

- The movement has become a symbol of civil society's power in India. After being widely televised by the Indian media, and widely supported by almost every Indian citizen (as the issue of corruption has been an issue every Indian holds very negative views about), the movement has attained a certain level of credibility in the eyes of the Indian masses.

- Its uniqueness in the fact that it was completely apolitical; was a movement solely of the people; did not wish to put in disarray the country as in the case of total shutdowns organised by political parties; and was able to bend the government—is something new for India.

- Many commentators have called the movement the 'wake-up' call for India.

- Meanwhile social networking chatter has been filled with fears that Indians will once again go back to 'sleep' with time.

Drafting Committee of the Bill

The 10 members Drafting Committee of the Jan Lokpal Bill will have an equal representation of both politicians and civil society members. On 8 April 2011, the Ministry of Law and Justice issued an official notification, The Gazette of India, regarding the Joint Drafting Committee of the bill. A copy of the notification can be found here:

Chairmen

The Government of India accepted that there be a politician Chairman and an activist, non-politician Co-Chairman. It is reported that Pranab Mukherjee, from the political arena, and Shanti Bhushan, from the civil society, will be the Chairmen of the Drafting Committee.

Government Representation

Five Cabinet ministers will be a part of the Drafting Committee. They are: Pranab Mukherjee, Finance Minister of India, Co-Chairman (with Shanti Bhushan); P. Chidambaram, Minister of Home Affairs, Panel Member; Veerappa Moily, Minister of Law and Justice, Panel Member; Kapil Sibal, Minister for Communications and Information Technology, Panel Member; Salman Khursid, Minister of Water Resources, Panel Member

Civil Society Representation

Five leading socialists will be a part of the Drafting Committee. They are: Shanti Bhushan, Former Minister of Law and Justice, Co-Chairman (with Pranab Mukherjee); Anna Hazare, Social Activist, Panel Members: Prashant Bhushan, Lawyer, N. Santosh Hegde, Lokayukta (Karnataka), Arvind Kejriwal, RTI activist.

Panel's Work to be Transparent

Anna Hazare has strongly proposed that proceedings of the joint committee should be video recorded when it starts the process of drafting the Lokpal Bill from April 16. "Nothing should be hidden from the people whose unstinted support led to the formation of the joint committee. I am also for total transparency till the Bill is enacted and also during the selection of the proposed Lokpal," Hazare said at a press conference on 10 April 2011.

He explained that he decided to go on a fast because the issue of Lokpal had remained undecided for 42 long years. He said, "On as many as eight occasions, the Lokpal Bill was introduced in Parliament but nothing happened. Now some people say this is blackmail. I will continue to indulge in such blackmail till I am alive because this is for the people's good. Hazare said he was confident that the drafting committee, comprising five senior ministers and five civil society members, would go by the principle of consensus while scripting the Bill. "The government has promised to introduce the Bill in Parliament by June 30. We will once again take to the protest path if it is not enacted within a reasonable time," he said, referring to his August 15 deadline.

State Bows to the Street Power

B. Raman, Former Additional Secretary (Govt. of India), and presently, Director, Institute for Topical Studies (Chennai) writes in the *Outlook* magazine (9 April 2011): "If there is one individual who has to be blamed for the success of street power over state power as a consequence of the national movement against corruption launched by social activist Anna Hazare, that individual has to be our Prime Minister, Dr Manmohan Singh. His government had been confronted with a series of serious allegations of corruption since the middle of last year—many of them true and some still under investigation. The relentless exposure of these instances of major corruption by the electronic media called for a leadership and communication skills of very high quality to reassure the public in a convincing manner that these allegations were being treated with all the seriousness they deserved and would be investigated thoroughly and action taken against those found guilty whatever be the position in public life occupied by them and whatever be the consequences to his continuance as the Prime Minister and to the stability and durability of the coalition government headed by him."

He explains further, "Instead of doing so, he handled these allegations in a halting manner that seemed not serious to the public of the country. There was a suspected attempt to keep the investigation pro forma instead of thorough-going and act against the wrong-doers only when forced to do so by the public campaign on this issue. Instead of accepting responsibility for what had gone wrong with an expression of his determination to root out this cancer, he constantly tried to blame the constraints of coalition politics for what had happened and gave an impression to the public of being weak and helpless. The nation desperately needed a cool and courageous captain who could control the ship of state after it had hit the iceberg of corruption. Instead what it had was a low-grade sailor who didn't seem to know how to steer the ship."

B. Raman writes, "The public was totally bewildered. It did not know what was happening as serious allegations of corruption came out one after the other from the news channels. Instead of interacting with the public directly and through his policy advisers and media managers in order to keep it informed of the real facts of the cases and to restore its shattered confidence in his administration, he withdrew into the fortress of the Prime Minister's office and avoided as far as possible interactions with the public and the media. One would have expected him to address the public through the TV and the radio in order to restore its confidence in the state. One would have thought that he would interact more frequently, more vigorously and more transparently with the media in order to regain his credibility and that of his government. Instead, he avoided interactions with the media and left this important task to his ministers of varying shades of seniority and credibility. His media managers, instead of acting as the facilitators of interactions with the media, saw themselves as controllers of his interactions with the media. Instead of encouraging him to boldly face the media and the public on this subject; they protected him from any unnecessary and unwise exposure to the media and the public."

"...The cumulative effect of the cascading instances of corruption and incompetence was the weakening of the credibility of the Prime Minister, a widening trust deficit between the government and the public and spreading anger and disgust over the unbridled corruption and the Prime Minister's perceived inability to deal with it. Into this messy situation walked a group of non-governmental activists led by Anna Hazare, who were hailed by growing sections of the public, particularly the youth, as the liberators of the people from the clutches of corruption and incompetence. They exploited the reluctance of successive governments for over 40 years to initiate action for setting up an independent institutional mechanism for dealing with corruption to rally the people around their flag for achieving a single demand—the setting-up of the independent institutional mechanism. ... The Prime Minister and his advisers totally misread the situation. They were surprised by the support of all sections of the people for this demand. They were taken aback by the youth coming out into the streets all over the country to support Anna Hazare. They were without answer to the triumvirate of forces that had joined hands in the name of a people's movement—the social activists led by Anna Hazare, self-motivated and angry students coming from different classes of society and the TV news channels."

Narendra Modi's Open Letter to Anna

A day after Anna Hazare praised Narendra Modi for the development work the Gujarat Chief Minister had undertaken, Modi posted (11 April 2011) an open letter on his blog addressed to Anna Hazare, hailing the veteran Gandhian and anti-corruption activist. Here's the full text of Narendra Modi's open letter to Anna Hazare:

My heartfelt feelings in an open letter to Annaji

Respected Annaji,

On the eighth day of fasting in the Navratri I am inspired to write to you early at 5 o'clock in the morning.

When you were sitting at fast in Delhi during that period, I too was fasting on the occasion of Navratri, the period that symbolizes the embodiment of Divine Shakti. I was pleased indeed that by the grace of Maa Jagadamba I happened to be a co-traveller in your crusade albeit indirectly.

Observing the Navratri fast and being busy in election campaigning, I was fortunate to have the darshan of Mother Kamakshi in Assam. Your fasting was in progress and naturally I did pray to Kamakshidevi about your health and I feel certain that a divine power has been kind enough to bestow her blessings on you.

Yesterday I was back from Kerala campaign to Gandhinagar at 2 A.M.

And it was yesterday that I got the encouraging news of your expressing kind words for Gujarat and me.

I am fortunate and grateful to get your blessings.

Respected Annaji, my respect for you is decades old. Before I entered politics I was full time RSS pracharak. At that time national leaders of the RSS who came to attend our meetings invariably discussed your rural development activities so that it could be emulated. It has tremendous impact on me. In the past I also had the good fortune of meeting you.

I and my state of Gujarat are indebted to you for the courage and conviction you showed in saying good words for me and my state. In this show of courage you exhibited commitment to truth and a soldier-like conviction. And because of this your opinion has been universally accepted.

I request you to also bless me that your praise will not make me complacent and commit mistakes.

Your blessings have given me the strength to do what is right and what is good. At the same time my responsibility has also become more. Because of your statement crores of youth would now be having great expectations and therefore even a small mistake of mine will disappoint them. Therefore I have to remain vigilant and I seek your blessings for the same.

Respected Annaji, in this delicate moment, I should say that I come from a simple family and am a common man too. In my family no one is even distantly connected to politics or remains close to power; I do not have illusions that I am a perfect individual. Like a common man I too have my own limitations; good and bad qualities.

I pray that I am always blessed by Mother Jagadamba so that bad qualities do not take possession of me. Always thinking of doing good to Gujarat, I would devote myself to the progress of Gujarat and therefore like to wipe out the tears from the face of the poor. For doing all this I pray that I am never short of your blessings, and this is my humble request.

Respected Annaji, you are a Gandhian and a soldier. Yesterday during election campaign in Kerala when I heard about your blessings for me and my state I feared that you will be subjected to vilification. A certain group inimical to Gujarat will not let go this opportunity to malign your love, sacrifice, penance and commitment to truth. They will try to tarnish your name because you spoke well of me and my state.

As bad luck would have it this has come true. Once again these inimical forces have come to the fore. On the occasion of Navratri I pray to Maa Jagadamba that no one sullies your fair name.

You will be aware that whosoever talks good of Gujarat he or she will be subjected to the vilification campaign.

In the past a senior Muslim parliamentarian from Canoor constituency hailing from the Communist Party Shri P. Abdulla Kutty was ostracized from the party following his praising of Gujarat's development.

The superstar of this century Shri Amitabh Bachchan when he worked free for Gujarat Tourism was also attacked by this same group of inimical forces. They spread falsehoods against Bachchan so as to snap his old ties with Gujarat. At a public function in Mumbai where Bachchan was invited this group had stopped him from entering.

Also a campaign was let loose to malign the leading Gandhian of Gujarat Shri Gunavant Shah who is speaking for the atma-gaurav of Gujarat.

Maulana Ghulam Vastanavi of Gujarat who was elected as head of the Darul Uloom of Deoband was also subjected to vilification campaign when he praised the development of Gujarat. He had publicly said that Gujarat is surging ahead on the road of fast paced development, and without any religious discrimination everybody was getting the fruits of development. Soon he was silenced by undue harassment by the same forces.

Recently, Major General I.S. Sinha (sic) of Golden Katara

division of Indian Army when he praised the development of Gujarat he too was beleaguered by the same forces and there was even a demand for disciplinary action against the major general.

These are only a few examples. But Gujarat's real developmental journey is an anathema to this group bent upon heaping calumny on my state. Whenever the name of Gujarat is mentioned these forces immediately swing into action to spread canards and falsehoods.

Respected Annaji, Gujarat's six crore people do not want that, the same group should sadden you.

I am still afraid that, this group will put you in trouble. May God give you strength.

I humbly bow to the sacrifices and penances you have made for the country. Let God bless you with supreme health so that many like me would be beneficiary of your guidance. This is my heartfelt prayer.

Yours

(Narendra Modi)

CHAPTER 2

Corruption in India

India has seen a lot of corruption in the last 60 years since independence. The economy of India was under socialist-inspired policies for an entire generation from the 1950s until the late 1980s. The economy was subject to extensive regulation, protectionism, and public ownership, leading to pervasive corruption and slow growth. License Raj was often at the core of corruption.

A 2005 study done by Transparency International in India found that more than 15 percent of the people in India had firsthand experience of paying bribe or peddling influence to get any type of job done in a public office. Taxes and bribes are a daily life fact, common between state borders; Transparency International estimates that truckers pay annually US$5 billion in bribes. For 2010, India was ranked 87th of 178 countries in Transparency International's Corruption Perceptions Index. As of 2010, India is amongst the most corrupt governments in the world, though one of the least corrupt in South Asia.[India needs to deal with the malice of corruption and improve governance in Asia's third-largest economy, Prime Minister Manmohan Singh said on 18 March 2011.

India tops the list for black money in the entire world with almost US$1456 billion in Swiss banks (US$1.4 trillion approximately) in the form of black money. According to the data provided by the Swiss Banking Association Report (2006), India has more black money than the rest of the world combined. Indian Swiss bank account assets are worth 13 times the country's national debt. Indian black money is sometimes physically transferred abroad. The CEO of a Mumbai-based equity firm recently told journalists that the money is flown abroad in "special flights" out of Mumbai and Delhi airports to Zurich. Indeed Indians would be the largest depositors of illegal money in Swiss banks, according to sources in the banking industry. The estimated average amount stashed away annually from India during 2002-06 is $27.3 billion US dollars.

Criminalisation of Indian politics is a serious problem. [In July 2008 *The Washington Post* reported that nearly a fourth of the 540 Indian Parliament members faced criminal charges. An international watchdog conducted a study on the illicit flight of money from India, perhaps the first ever attempt at shedding light on a subject steeped in secrecy, concludes that India has been drained of $462 billion (over Rs 20 lakh crore) between 1948 and 2008. The amount is nearly 40 percent of India's annual gross domestic product.

Independent reports, particularly by S. Gurumurthy (Published by *The New Indian Express*, January 2, 2011) have recently calculated India's traditionally ruling political-family's (Gandhi's) net worth to be anywhere between Rs. 42,345 crore (US$ 9.4 billion) to Rs. 83,900 crore (US$18.63 billion), most of it in the form of illegal monies.

Harvard scholar Yevgenia Albats cited KGB correspondence about payments to Rajiv Gandhi and his family, which had been arranged by Viktor Chebrikov, which shows that KGB chief

Viktor Chebrikov sought in writing an "authorisation to make payments in US dollars to the family members of Rajiv Gandhi, namely Sonia Gandhi, Rahul Gandhi and Paola Maino, mother of Sonia Gandhi" from the CPSU in December 1985.

The organisers of Dandi March II in the United States said: "The recent scams involving unimaginably big amounts of money, such as the 2G spectrum scam, are well known. It is estimated that more than trillion dollars are stashed away in foreign havens, while 80 percent of Indians earn less than 2$ per day and every second child is malnourished. It seems as if only the honest people are poor in India and want to get rid of their poverty by education, emigration to cities, and immigration, whereas all the corrupt ones, like Hasan Ali Khan are getting rich through scams and crime. It seems as if India is a rich country filled with poor people."

Despite this, Government of India is sitting on unused foreign aid of over Rs.100,000 crore (US$ 22.2 billion) reflecting inadequate planning by ministries like urban development, water resources and energy, a report by government auditor Comptroller and Auditor General of India (CAG) has said. "As on March 31, 2010, unutilised committed external assistance was of the order of Rs.1,05,339 crore," the CAG said in its report tabled in Parliament on 18 March 2011. In fact, the Indian government has paid commitment charges of Rs. 86.11 crore (US$19.12 million) out of taxpayer-money during 2009-10 in the form of penalty for not timely utilising the aid approved by multilateral and bilateral lending agencies.

Major Scams After 1991

According to the *Outlook* Magazine (Published 23 November 2009), the opening up of the Indian Economy in 1991 boosted scam monies into the stratosphere. A conservative listing by

Outlook of financial scams since 1991 has pegged the money looted at a mind-boggling Rs 73 lakh crore. Listing by the magazine as follows:

1992   Harshad Mehta securities scam Rs 5,000 crore

1994   Sugar import scam Rs 650 crore

1995   Preferential allotment scam Rs 5,000 crore; Yugoslav Dinar scam Rs 400 crore; Meghalaya Forest scam Rs 300 crore

1996   Fertiliser import scam Rs 1,300 crore; Urea scam Rs 133 crore; Bihar fodder scam Rs 950 crore

1997   Sukh Ram telecom scam Rs 1,500 crore; SNC Lavalin power project scam Rs 374 crore; Bihar land scandal Rs 400 crore; C.R. Bhansali stock scam Rs 1,200 crore

1998   Teak plantation swindle Rs 8,000 crore

2001   UTI scam Rs 4,800 crore; Dinesh Dalmia stock scam Rs 595 crore; Ketan Parekh securities scam Rs 1,250 crore

2002   Sanjay Agarwal Home Trade scam Rs 600 crore

2003   Telgi stamp paper scam Rs 172 crore

2005   IPO-Demat scam Rs 146 crore; Bihar flood relief scam Rs 17 crore; Scorpene submarine scam Rs 18,978 crore

2006   Punjab's City Centre project scam Rs 1,500 crore, Taj Corridor scam Rs 175 crore

2008   Pune billionaire Hassan Ali Khan tax default Rs 50,000 crore; The Satyam scam Rs 10,000 crore; Army ration pilferage scam Rs 5,000 crore; The 2-G spectrum swindle Rs 60,000 crore; State Bank of Saurashtra scam Rs 95 crore; Illegal monies in Swiss banks, as estimated in 2008 Rs 71,00,000 crore.

2009   The Jharkhand medical equipment scam Rs 130

crore; Rice export scam Rs 2,500 crore; Orissa mine scam Rs 7,000 crore; Madhu Koda mining scam Rs 4,000 crore

Since 1991, when the Indian economy was opened up to make way for reforms—reforms that were aimed at unshackling the licence raj and reducing the scope for corruption—financial scams have ironically become the norm. Talking to the magazine, Professor Arun Kumar of Delhi's Jawaharlal Nehru University, says, "The usual has become the unusual and the unusual the usual." Kumar points out that between 1991-96, just after liberalisation, there were as many as 26 cases. Of these, 13 involved more than a thousand crore each. The number of zeroes have only kept increasing since, pushing scam amounts to astronomical sums. The spectrum allotment scam of '08 is reportedly worth Rs 60,000 crore—that's the kind of territory we routinely inhabit now.

Kumar believes the present size of the black economy in India is as high as 50 per cent (Rs 26,60,876.5 crore) of the country's GDP. This figure, of course, is all-inclusive, and will count anybody who does not pay tax for an income earned, even the school teacher who does not declare his after-school tuitions. According to Kumar, in the '50s this parallel economy was only five per cent of the GDP. Ironically, it is the urge to promote business and development at any cost that has bred this level of corruption.

Talking to the magazine E.A.S. Sarma, former secretary of the department of economic affairs, says, "In the fast-track clearance paradigm, the government is prepared to look the other way when a developer violates established norms. And if any law comes in the way, it is prepared to rush and dilute them." The capital markets post-liberalisation—often feted for the swinging highs they produce, almost as if it's an index of the country's economic health—are themselves flawed because adequate supervision, strict accountability and appropriate punishment are still missing, writes noted business journalist Sucheta Dalal.

The nexus between money and politics is also undergoing a shift with the former gaining the upper hand. Referring to the recent spate of money-tinged political scams—including those involving Madhu Koda, Union telecom minister A. Raja and the Reddy brothers of Bellary—Jayaprakash Narayan of the Lok Satta Party in AP points out that they "dramatically" demonstrate the next phase of this relationship. "It is no longer politics being just influenced by money. Today, it's actually dictating terms," he says. "There's no wealth creation. The state's natural resources are given away arbitrarily to private parties, the only consideration being the *mala fide* intent of building private empires."

The CPI's A.B. Bardhan agrees: "The power of big money hovers like a dark cloud over our democracy. Crores are being spent on elections, even those to elect ward representatives. This keeps the poor and the parties of the poor from contesting elections successfully. Koda may have been caught but there are many big fish who have not been. For instance, it's been reported that the average worth of the re-elected Haryana MLA has grown by Rs 5 crore. Even Jaganmohan Reddy's assets are said to have jumped manifold. How do you explain it? This influence of money on democracy is eating into our moral fibre. We are in the midst of a moral crisis where very many people think corruption is now natural and normal."

The failure to act on corruption is almost systemic—with a few exceptions, politicians by and large have not been brought to book. Even the judiciary hasn't escaped the corruption taint— an allegation of land-grabbing against the Karnataka High Court Chief Justice P.D. Dinakaran is a recent case in point. Another check—the bureaucracy—had even earlier fallen prey to corruption and there are few insiders willing to speak out. But there are some who are not so skeptical. R.H. Tahiliani, a retired admiral, Chairman of Transparency International India, talking with *Outlook* magazine, says, "Corruption is at its apex in the electoral system. One therefore can't let go of the politicians, more so because the tone is set by the rulers ... water at 99 degree Celsius is hot but it has no energy. Add a degree, it starts boiling, develops steam and gains tremendous energy. Just like that, those against corruption need to keep up the struggle. You never know when those few extra degrees may come. After all, the Berlin Wall still came down without a single shot being fired, didn't it?"

Indian Political Scandals

Churhat Lottery Case (1982)

While Arjun Singh was the Chief Minister of Madhya Pradesh, he was involved in the scandal which was called by some the Churhat Lottery case. The Churhat Children Welfare Society was floated in 1982 by relatives of Singh, and permitted to raise funds via lottery, and also given tax relief as a charity. However, there were widespread allegations that a substantial sum were siphoned off and used to construct the lavish Kerwa Dam palace near Bhopal. The donations to the society included Rs 150,000 donation from Union Carbide, whose chief Warren Anderson was permitted to leave the country after the gas leak, allegedly by Arjun Singh's office.

At a public litigation hearing the high court observed that "Arjun Singh owed an explanation to the nation about the costs and sources of construction of the palatial mansion in Bhopal". While Singh had claimed the value of the palace was Rs 18 lakh, the IT Department estimated the cost at above Rs one crore. However, a one-judge commission investigating the scandal gave a clean chit to Arjun Singh. The case was re-opened however, after the Jain Hawala case, and Singh was asked to submit fresh re-estimates of the palace cost. In court, the case was argued by Kapil Sibal and the order for re-examination was squashed on the grounds that it had been issued in haste and "had not applied his mind."

St Kitts Case (1989)

P.V. Narsimha Rao, along with fellow minister K.K. Tewary, Chandraswami and K.N. Aggarwal were accused of forging documents showing that Ajeya Singh had opened a bank account in the First Trust Corporation Bank in St. Kitts and deposited $21 million in it, making his father V.P. Singh its beneficiary. The alleged intent was to tarnish V.P. Singh's image. This supposedly happened in 1989. However only after Rao's term as PM had expired in 1996, he was formally charged by the Central Bureau of Investigation for the crime. Less than a year later the court acquitted him due to lack of evidence linking him with the case. All the other accused, Chandraswami being the last, were also eventually acquitted.

Bofors Scandal (1987)

The Bofors scandal, a major corruption scandal in India, broke out 1987; the then Prime Minister Rajiv Gandhi and several others were accused of receiving kickbacks from Bofors AB for winning a bid to supply India's 155 mm field howitzer. The scale of the corruption was far worse than any that India had seen before, and directly led to the defeat of Gandhi's ruling Indian National Congress party in the November 1989 general elections. It has been speculated that the scale of the scandal was to the tune of Rs. 400 million. The case came to light during Vishwanath Pratap Singh's tenure as Defence Minister, and was revealed through investigative journalism by Chitra

Subramaniam and N. Ram of the *Indian Express* and *The Hindu*, two leading Indian dailies.

The name of the middleman associated with the scandal was Ottavio Quattrocchi, an Italian businessman who represented the petrochemicals firm Snamprogetti. Quattrocchi was reportedly close to the family of Prime Minister Rajiv Gandhi and emerged as a powerful broker in the 1980s between big businesses and the Indian government. While the case was being investigated, Rajiv Gandhi was assassinated on May 21, 1991 for an unrelated cause. In 1997, the Swiss banks released some 500 documents after years of legal battle and the Central Bureau of Investigation (CBI) filed a case against Quattrocchi, Win Chadha, also naming Rajiv Gandhi, the defence secretary S.K. Bhatnagar and a number of others. In the meantime, Win Chadha also died.

Meanwhile February 5, 2004, the Delhi High Court quashed the charges of bribery against Rajiv Gandhi and others, but the case is still being tried on charges of cheating, causing wrongful loss to the government, etc. On May 31, 2005, the High Court of Delhi dismissed the Bofors case allegations against the British businessmen brothers, Shrichand, Gopichand and Prakash Hinduja

In December 2005, the Mr B. Daat, the additional solicitor general of India, acting on behalf of the Indian Government and the CBI, requested the British Government that two British bank accounts of Ottavio Quattrocchi be unfrozen on the grounds of insufficient evidence to link these accounts to the Bofors payoff. The two accounts, containing • 3 million and $1 million, had been frozen. On January 16, the Indian Supreme Court directed the Indian government to ensure that Ottavio Quattrocchi did not withdraw money from the two bank accounts in London. The CBI, the Indian federal law enforcement agency, on January 23, 2006 admitted that roughly Rs 21 crore, about US $4.6 million, in the two accounts have already been withdrawn. The British government released the funds based on a request by the Indian government. The deals cost the Government of India an extra 160 crore rupees.

However, on January 16, 2006, CBI claimed in an affidavit filed before the Supreme Court that they were still pursuing extradition orders for Quattrocchi. The Interpol, at the request of the CBI, has a long-standing red corner notice to arrest Quattrocchi. Quattrocchi was detained in Argentina on 6 February 2007, but the news of his detention was released by the CBI only on 23 February. Quattrocchi has been released by Argentinian police. However, his passport was impounded and he was not allowed to leave the country.

However, as there was no extradition treaty between India and Argentina, the case was presented in the Argentine Supreme Court. The government of India lost the extradition case as the government of India did not provide a key court order which was the basis of Quattrochi's arrest. In the aftermath, the government did not appeal this decision owing delays in securing an official English translation of the court's decision. The Italian businessman no longer figures in the CBI's list of wanted persons and the 12-year Interpol red corner notice against the lone surviving suspect in the Bofors payoff case has been withdrawn from the agency's website after the CBI's appeal. A Delhi court discharged Quattrocchi from the case, as there was no credible evidence against him, on 4 March 2011.

JMM Bribery Scandal (1993)

In July 1993, Rao's government was facing a no-confidence motion, because the opposition felt that it did not have sufficient numbers to prove a majority. It was alleged that Rao, through a representative, offered millions of rupees to members of the Jharkhand Mukti Morcha (JMM), and possibly a breakaway faction of the Janata Dal, to vote for him during the confidence motion. Shailendra Mahato, one of those members who had accepted the bribe, turned approver. In 1996, after Rao's term in office had expired, investigations began in earnest in the case. In 2000, after years of legal proceedings, a special court convicted Rao and his colleague, Buta Singh (who is alleged to have escorted the MPs to the Prime Minister). Rao appealed to a higher court and remained free on bail. The decision was overturned mainly due to the doubt in credibility of Mahato's statements (which were extremely inconsistent) and both Rao and Buta Singh were cleared of the charges in 2002.

Hawala Scam (1993)

It was an Indian political scandal involving payments allegedly received by politicians through hawala brokers, the Jain brothers. It was a US$18 million bribery scandal that broke out in 1993. With some of the country's leading politicians, 115 top bureaucrats were identified as having participated in the scam. There were also alleged connections with payments being channelled to Hizbul Mujahideen militants in Kashmir.

The case got a momentary boost up as a result of a PIL (Public Interest Litigation) filed in the Supreme Court, by Vineet Narain, the journalist who broke the story. In 1996 for the first time in Indian history, several cabinet ministers, chief ministers and governors were charge-sheeted. Those accused included L.K. Advani, V.C. Shukla, P. Shiv Shankar, Sharad Yadav, Balram Jakhar, and Madan Lal Khurana. Many were acquitted in 1997 and 1998, partly because the hawala records (including diaries) were judged in court to be inadequate as the main evidence. The failure of this prosecution by the Central Bureau of Investigation was widely criticised.

The Fodder Scam (1996)

It was a corruption scandal that involved the alleged embezzlement of about Rs. 950 crore (US$210.9 million) from the government treasury of the Indian state of Bihar. The alleged theft spanned many years, was engaged in by many Bihar state government administrative and elected officials across multiple administrations (run by opposing political parties), and involved the fabrication of "vast herds of fictitious livestock" for which fodder, medicines and animal husbandry equipment was supposedly procured. Although the scandal broke in 1996, the theft had been in progress, and increasing in size, for over two decades.

A Public Interest Litigation (PIL) was filed with the Supreme Court of India, which led to the court's involvement, and based on the ultimate directions issued by the Supreme Court, on March 1996; the Bihar High Court ordered that the case be handed over to the CBI. The CBI unearthed linkages to the serving chief minister of Bihar, Laloo Prasad Yadav and, on May 10, 1997, made a formal request to the governor of Bihar to prosecute Laloo. On the same day, a businessman, Harish Khandelwal, who was one of the accused, was found dead on train tracks with a note that stated that he was being coerced by the CBI to turn witness for the prosecution.

On June 17, the governor gave permission for Laloo and others to be prosecuted. On June 23, the CBI filed charge sheets against Laloo and 55 other co-accused, including Chandradeo Prasad Verma (a former union minister), Jagannath Mishra (former Bihar chief minister), two members of Laloo's cabinet (Bhola Ram Toofani and Vidya Sagar Nishad), three Bihar state assembly legislators (R.K. Rana of the Janata Dal, Jagdish Sharma of the Congress party, and Dhruv Bhagat of the Bharatiya Janata Party) and some current and former IAS officers (including the 4 who were already in custody). Mishra was granted anticipatory bail by the Bihar state High Court. Laloo's anticipatory bail petition, however, was rejected by the same court, and he appealed to the Supreme Court, which resulted in a final denial of bail on July 29. On the same day, Bihar state police were ordered to arrest him. The next day, he was jailed.

With demands for his resignation continuing to mount, on July 25, Laloo resigned from his position, but was able to install his wife, Rabri Devi as the new chief minister on the same day. On July 28, Rabri's new government successfully won another trust vote in the Bihar legislature by a 194-110 vote, thanks to the Congress and Jharkhand Mukti Morcha parties voting in alignment with the RJD. In between On June 30, the federal government issued orders to transfer Director Joginder Singh out of the CBI and into the Home Ministry as a Special Secretary, which was technically a promotion but also had the effect of removing him from the investigation. There was also an alleged follow-on move to transfer UN Biswas, the regional CBI director, which led to the High Court warning that it would act to disallow any such transfer.

Due to the multiplicity of cases, Laloo Yadav, Jagannath Mishra, and the other accused have been remanded several times in the years since 2000. In 2007, 58 former officials and suppliers were convicted, and given terms of 5 to 6 years each. As of May 2007, about 200 people had been punished with jail terms of between 2 and 7 years.

Telecom-Sukh Ram-Scam (1996)

Two cases were filed against Sukh Ram, the then Union Communications Minister, after suitcases stuffed with cash were seized from his houses in New Delhi and Mandi in August 1996. He was a member of Lok Sabha from Mandi constituency of

Himachal Pradesh. He has a record of winning Vidhan sabha elections five times and Lok sabha elections three times.

He, now 84, is still doing the rounds of the courts. The case in which he was convicted of amassing over Rs 4 crore disproportionate assets during his tenure in the Narasimha Rao government is still pending in the Delhi High Court, after an appeal was filed in 2009. In the second case, Sukh Ram was convicted in 2002. He was sentenced to three years' rigorous imprisonment for causing a loss of Rs 1.66 crore to the exchequer by favouring a private firm, Advance Radio Masts (ARM) Pvt Ltd, in the purchase of telecom equipment. He was also fined Rs 2 lakh.

Barak Missile Scandal (2001)

It is a case of defence corruption relating to the purchase of Barak Missile Systems by India from Israel. The case is currently under investigation by the Central Bureau of Investigation, and several people including the Samata Party ex-treasurer R.K. Jain have been arrested. Others named in the First Information Report include politicians George Fernandes and Jaya Jaitley, and arms dealer and ex-naval officer Suresh Nanda, who is the son of retired Chief of Naval Staff S.M. Nanda.

The Barak missile system (jointly developed by Israel Aircraft Industries (IAI) and RAFAEL Armament Development Authority of Israel) employs vertically launched missiles to counter anti-ship sea-skimming missiles and attacks by aircraft. On October 23, 2000, contracts had been signed by the Indian government to procure seven Barak systems at a total cost $199.50 million and 200 missiles at a cost of $69.13 million. This was done despite objections raised by several groups, including members of the team that had originally visited Israel to observe the missile performance, and APJ Abdul Kalam, then heading the Defence Research Development Organisation. Though some of the objections are of a procedural nature, the Navy Chief of Staff Sushil Kumar is currently under investigation as to why these objections were not considered.

In 2001 a sting operation conducted by Tehelka, alleged that 15 defence deals made by the government had involved some sort of kickbacks and the Barak missile deal was one of them.

Tehelka claimed to have filmed Bangaru Laxman (the secretary of the ruling party BJP) taking a bribe for helping the bogus company in procuring government contracts. During the process, Tehelka also met Jaya Jaitley, the head of Samata Party and a close aide of the defence minister George Fernandes. There was an outcry when the scandal broke, and George Fernandes resigned although he was not accused of taking bribe. Laxman also resigned, while Jaya Jaitly accused Tehelka journalists of being Pakistani agents and raised doubts over the authenticity of the tapes. The tapes were sent to UK for forensic examination, and were confirmed as genuine.

Fernandes returned to power soon afterwards, and the inquiry set up to investigate the charges halted upon the resignation of the sitting judge, while his replacement performed an ineffectual job lacking in focus. The government turned the tables on Tehelka with an investigation into its conduct. The main financial backers of Tehelka were made targets of investigations from the customs, the police and the tax authorities. By 2003, the number of salaried employees in the company had reduced from 120 to 1, and the company was practically ruined. The investigations against the MoD officials were revived in 2004, when the Congress-led government came to the power and handed over the matter to the Central Bureau of Investigation (CBI).

Madhu Koda Money-laundering Scam

On 10 October 2009, Madhu Koda, than Chief Minister of Jharkhand, was charged with laundering money worth over Rs. 4000 crores. In nationwide raids by the Enforcement Directorate, assets allegedly worth Rs. 4000 crore—almost a fifth of the annual budget of the state he once ruled—were unearthed. Among others, these assets were reported to include hotels and three companies in Mumbai, property in Kolkata, a hotel in Thailand, and a coal mine in Liberia. On of his two close associates Binod Sinha is behind bars, and Sanjay Chowdhary has escaped to Dubai. Madu Koda is spending his time in jail like any other prisoner of the Birsa Munda Central Jail at Hotwar.

Madhu Koda (born January 6, 1971) was sworn in as the fifth Chief Minister of Jharkhand on September 18, 2006 and remained in office until he resigned on 23 August 2008; he was succeeded by Shibu Soren. He began his political career as an activist with the All Jharkhand Students Union. He won in the 2000 Assembly elections from Jaganathpur as a Bharatiya Janata Party (BJP) candidate. In the government headed by Chief Minister Babulal Marandi, Madhu became the Panchayati Raj Minister. He subsequently held this post when Arjun Munda took over the reins in 2003.

During the 2005 Assembly Elections in Jharkhand, the BJP denied Koda a ticket. He contested as an Independent candidate and won from Jaganathpur once again, defeating his nearest rival from the Indian National Congress by over ten thousand votes. With a fractured mandate in the state, Koda agreed to support a BJP-led government led by Arjun Munda, taking over as the Minister of Mines and Geology. In September 2006, Madhu and three other independent legislators withdrew support to the Munda government, bringing it into the minority. In the subsequent period, the opposition United Progressive Alliance decided on him as consensus candidate to become Chief Minister.

2G Spectrum Scam

The 2G spectrum scam involved officials and ministers in the Government of India illegally undercharging mobile telephony companies for frequency allocation licenses, which they would use to create 2G subscriptions for cell phones. According to a report submitted by the Comptroller and Auditor General based on money collected from 3G licenses, the loss to the exchequer was Rs.176,379 crores (US$39.16 billion).

The issuing of the 2G licenses occurred in 2008, but the scam came to public notice when the Indian Income Tax Department investigated political lobbyist Nira Radia and the Supreme Court of India took Subramaniam Swamy's complaints on record. Former Telecom Minister of the NDA government Arun Shourie was the whistleblower who helped uncover the scam and also exposed many loopholes in the UPA government's policy towards issuing telecom licences.

In 2008, the Income Tax department, after orders from the ministry of Home and the PMO, began tapping the phones of Nira Radia. This was done to help with an ongoing investigation into a case where it was alleged that Niira Radia had acted as a spy. Some of the many conversations recorded over 300 days were leaked to the media. The intense controversy around the leaked tapes became known in the media as the Radia tapes controversy. The tapes featured some conversations between politicians, journalists and corporation. Politicians like Karunanidhi, journalists like Barkha Dutt, Vir Sanghvi and Prabhu Chawla and industrial groups like the Tata Group were either participants or mentioned in these tapes.

Raja arranged the sale of the 2G spectrum licenses below their market value. Swan Telecom, a new company with few assets, bought a license for Rs.1,537 crore (US$341.21 million). Shortly thereafter, the board sold 45 percent of the company to Etisalat for Rs.4,200 crore (US$932.4 million). Similarly, a company formerly invested in real estate and not telecom, the Unitech Group, purchased a license for Rs.1,661 crore (US$368.74 million) and the company board soon after sold a 60 percent stake in their wireless division for Rs. 6,200 crore (US$1.38 billion) to Telenor.

The nature of the selling of the licenses was that licenses were to be sold at market value, and the fact that the licenses were quickly resold at a huge profit indicates that the selling agents were issued the licenses below market value. Nine companies purchased licenses and collectively they paid the Ministry of Communications and Information Technology's telecom-munications division Rs.10,772 crore (US$2.39 billion). The amount of money expected for this licensing by the Comptroller and Auditor General of India was Rs.176,700 crore (US$39.23 billion).

In early November 2010, Jayalalithaa accused the Tamil Nadu state chief minister M. Karunanidhi of protecting A. Raja from corruption charges and called for A. Raja's resignation. By mid November A. Raja resigned. In mid-November, the comptroller Vinod Rai issued show-cause notices to Unitech, S Tel, Loop Mobile, Datacom (Videocon), and Etisalat to respond to his assertion that all of the 85 licenses granted to these companies did not have the up-front capital required at the time of the application and were in other ways illegal. Some media sources have speculated that these companies will receive large fines but not have their licenses revoked, as they are currently providing some consumer service.

In response to the various allegations, the Government of India has replaced the then incumbent Telecom minister, A. Raja with Kapil Sibal who has taken up this charge in addition to being the Union minister for Human Resources Development. Sibal contends that the "notional" losses quoted are a result of erroneous calculations and insists that the actual losses are nil.

The CBI conducted raids on A. Raja and four other telecom officials—former telecom secretary Siddharth Behura, Raja's personal secretary R.K. Chandolia, member telecom K. Sridhar and DoT deputy director general A.K. Srivastava on 8 December 2010. On February 2, 2011, the CBI arrested A. Raja, R.K. Chandolia, Raja's personal aide, and Siddharth Behura, the former Telecom Secretary. Both A. Raja and R.K. Chandolia are heard in conversation with Niira Radia in the released Radia tapes. On February 8, 2011, the CBI arrested Mumbai based Dynamix Balwas (DB) group managing director Shahid Usman Balwa in connection with the 2G spectrum allocation scam. The CBI has evidence from the Income Tax department that Shahid Usman Balwa, considered close to A. Raja, was instrumental in channelling the kickbacks allegedly received by the former telecom minister. On March 29, 2011, in Delhi, the CBI arrested Asif Balwa (younger brother of the arrested former Managing Director of DB-Etisalat Group, Shahid Balwa) and Rajeev Agarwal for their alleged involvement in money transfer to the Dravida Munnetra Kazhagam's (DMK) Kalaignar TVchannel.

On 2 April 2011, the CBI filed its first 80,000 page charge sheet in the 2G spectrum scam before a Special Court in Delhi naming nine individuals and three companies. It said the wrongful acts of the accused deprived the government exchequer of possible revenues amounting to Rs 30,985 crore. The accused include: A. Raja, arrested former Telecom minister; Siddharth

Behura, arrested former Telecom Secretary; R.K. Chandolia, A. Raja's arrested former personal secretary; Shahid Usman Balwa, arrested former Director of Swan Telecom (now Etisalat DB); Sanjay Chandra, Managing Director of Unitech Ltd and Unitech Wireless; Gautam Doshi, Group MD, Reliance Anil Dhirubhai Ambani Group; Hari Nair, Senior Vice-President, Reliance Anil Dhirubhai Ambani Group; Surendra Pipara, Senior Vice-President, Reliance Anil Dhirubhai Ambani Group and Reliance Telecom Ltd; Vinod Goenka, Director, Swan Telecom and Managing Director of DB Realty. The three companies named are: Swan Telecom, Unitech Wireless, and Reliance Telecom. In the first chargesheet, the CBI had named lobbyist Niira Radia and 124 others as witnesses.

Adarsh Housing Society Scam

The Adarsh Housing Society is a cooperative society in the city of Mumbai in India. It was reserved for the war widows and veterans of the Kargil War. In 2010, the Indian media brought to public the violations of rules at various phases of construction in the Adarsh Society. Questions were raised on the manner in which apartments in the building were allocated to bureaucrats, politicians and army personnel who had nothing to do with Kargil War and the way in which clearances were obtained for the construction of the building of the Adarsh Society.

The Adarsh society high-rise was constructed in the posh Colaba locality of Mumbai, which is considered a sensitive coastal area by the Indian Defence forces and houses various Indian Defense establishments. The society is also alleged to have violated the Indian environment ministry rules. Many activists like Medha Patkar had been trying to uncover this scam since a long time. The exposure of the infamous nexus between politicians, bureaucrats and builders in this scam is said to be only the tip of the iceberg. It had led to resignation of the then Chief Minister, Ashok Chavan.

Several inquiries have been ordered by the army and the Government to probe into the irregularities. Some of the current occupants of the flats in the Adarsh co-operative society building have offered to vacate their flats at the earliest, denying allegations that they were alloted flats because they influenced or helped, in some manner, the construction of the society by violating the rules. The media also exposed that the lower house of the Indian Parliament was misled by one of the bureaucrats, Pradeep Vyas, involved.

As per the Ministry of Environment and Forests order dated 16 January 2011, the unauthorised structure should be removed in its entirety and the area restored to its original condition.

CHAPTER 3

Laws and Actions Against Corruption

The stand-off between the government and social activist groups, now led by Anna Hazare, has brought the issue of the Lok Pal Bill to the forefront. The word Lokpal means an ombudsman in India. The word has been derived from the Hindi words "lok" (people) and "pal" (protector/caretaker). So the word Lokpal means 'protector of people'. The concept of Lokpal has been drawn up ostensibly to root out corruption at high places in the prevailing Indian polity.

The basic idea of the institution of Lok Pal was borrowed from the concept of Ombudsman in countries such as Finland, Norway, Denmark, Sweden, U.K. and New Zealand. In 1995, the European Union created the post of European Ombudsman. Presently, about 140 countries have the office of the Ombudsman. The Ombudsman is an institution, independent of the judiciary, executive and legislature and analogous with that of a high judicial functionary. He is mostly free to choose his investigation method and agency. The expenditure of the office is under Parliamentary control. In Sweden, Denmark and Finland, the office of the Ombudsman can redress citizens' grievances by either directly receiving complaint from the public or *suo moto*. However, in the UK, the office of the Parliamentary Commissioner can receive complaints only through Members of Parliament (to whom the citizen can complain). Sweden and Finland also have the power to prosecute erring public servants.

After 42 years, the Lokpal Bill is still pending in India. The first Lokpal Bill was passed in the 4th Lok Sabha in 1969 but could not get through in Rajya Sabha, subsequently, Lokpal Bills were introduced in 1971, 1977, 1985, 1989, 1996, 1998, 2001, 2005 and in 2008, yet they were never passed.

The Lokpal Bill provides for filing complaints of corruption against the prime minister, other ministers, and MPs with the ombudsman. The Administrative Reforms Commission (ARC) while recommending the constitution of Lokpal was convinced that such an institution was justified not only for removing the sense of injustice from the minds of adversely affected citizens but also necessary to instill public confidence in the efficiency of administrative machinery. Following this, the Lokpal Bill was for the first time presented during the fourth Lok Sabha in 1968, and was passed there in 1969.

However, while it was pending in the Rajya Sabha, the Lok Sabha was dissolved, resulting in the death of the first bill. The bill was revived in 1971, 1977, 1985, 1989, 1996, 1998, 2001, and 2005 and most recently in 2008. Each time, after the bill was introduced in the house, it was referred to some committee for improvements—a joint committee of parliament, or a departmental standing committee of the Home Ministry—and before the government could take a final stand on the issue, the house was dissolved. Several flaws have been cited in the recent draft of the Lokpal Bill.

Actions by Central Government

The central government has been considering the introduction of a Lok Pal Bill to put in place a mechanism to tackle corruption. Currently, public servants (such as government employees, judges, armed forces, police) can be prosecuted for corruption under the Indian Penal Code, 1860 and the Prevention of Corruption Act, 1988. However, the Code of Criminal Procedure and the Act require the investigating agency (such as CBI) to get prior sanction of the central or state government before it can initiate the prosecution process in a court.

The Supreme Court in the 1998 P.V. Narasimha Rao bribery case ruled that Members of Parliament (MPs) fall within the ambit of the definition of "public servant" in the Prevention of Corruption Act, 1988. However, opinion among the judges was divided over the issue of previous sanction with one side stating that MPs could not be prosecuted since there was no authority competent to give sanction and the other suggesting that till the law is suitably amended, the Speaker of the Lok Sabha and Chairman of the Rajya Sabha should give the necessary sanction.

The idea of constituting an Ombudsman type institution to look into the grievances of individuals against the administration was first mooted in 1963 during a debate on Demands for Grants for the Law Ministry. In 1966, the First Administrative Reforms Commission recommended that two independent authorities at the central and state level be established to enquire into complaints against public functionaries (including Members of Parliament).

The Lok Pal Bill was introduced for the first time in 1968 but it lapsed with the dissolution of the Lok Sabha. It was introduced seven more times in Parliament, the last time in

2001. However, the Bill lapsed each time except in 1985 when it was withdrawn. At the state level, so far 18 states have created the institution of the Lokayukta through the Lokayukta Acts.

In 2002, the report of the National Commission to Review the Working of the Constitution urged that the Constitution should provide for the appointment of the Lok Pal and Lokayuktas in the states but suggested that the Prime Minister should be kept out of the purview of the authority. In 2004, the UPA government's National Common Minimum Programme promised that the Lok Pal Bill would be enacted. The Second Administrative Commission, formed in 2005, also recommended that the office of the Lok Pal be established without delay. In January 2011, the government formed a Group of Ministers, chaired by Shri Pranab Mukherjee to suggest measures to tackle corruption, including examination of the proposal of a Lok Pal Bill.

A number of commissions have made recommendations on various aspects of the office of Lok Pal including procedure of appointment, powers of inquiry, and powers of prosecution.

First Administrative Reforms Commission (1966)
- A citizen has the right to seek redressal against administrative acts of the government. He can either move court or seek other remedies such as petitioning his Member of Parliament. However, these remedies are limited because they maybe too cumbersome or specific grievances may not be addressed. Therefore, a more effective and simpler machinery is required to redress specific grievances of citizens against the administration.
- Each government department should have a suitable machinery to receive and investigate complaints and set in motion the administrative process to provide remedies.

There should also be two independent authorities to redress grievances: (a) Lok Pal, which shall deal with complaints against the administrative acts of Ministers or secretaries of government at the centre and the state; and (b) Lokayukta in each state and at the centre, which would deal with complaints against the administrative acts of other officials.

- These authorities should be independent of the executive as well as the legislature and the judiciary. The Lok Pal should be appointed by the President on the advice of the Prime Minister. The PM shall consult the Chief Justice of India and the Leader of the Opposition. The Lok Pal shall have the same stature as the Chief Justice of India and can be removed only by impeachment. The Lokayuktas shall have similar powers as the Lok Pal and shall be equivalent to the Chief Justice of a High Court. Their appointment should, as far as possible, be non-political.

- The Lok Pal may either act on the complaints made by an affected citizen or on his own cognition. He shall investigate cases related to maladministration, which involves acts of injustice, corruption and favouritism. The investigations and proceedings should be conducted in private and should be informal.

- On receiving a complaint, the Lok Pal shall decide whether it is worth investigating, then send for comments to the concerned department. After getting the report, the Lok Pal shall decide if he wants to proceed or not. If he investigates and finds that injustice has been done, he shall suggest remedial action to the department. If the department does not act on it, he can report to the Prime Minister or the Chief Minister, who shall report back within two months. If he is not satisfied, then he may bring it to the notice of the Parliament or the Legislature. If there are criminal charges against a public official, he can bring it to the notice of the Prime Minister or the Chief Minister and they can then set the machinery of law in motion and inform the Lok Pal.

National Commission to Review the Working of the Constitution (2002)

- The Constitution should provide for the appointment of the Lok Pal. But the office of the Prime Minister should be kept out of the purview of the Lok Pal.
- Its findings should be final and form the basis for action by the government.
- The Constitution should make it obligatory for states to establish the institution of Lokayuktas.
- The Constitution should be amended to state that Members of Parliament may be prosecuted for the offence of giving or receiving monetary or other valuable considerations for voting in a particular manner or not voting.
- An MP can be prosecuted after the investigating agency receives prior sanction from a committee constituted by the President. The committee shall have five MPs, nominated by the President in consultation with the Speaker of the Lok Sabha and the Chairman of the Rajya Sabha.

Second Administrative Reforms Commission (2007)

Lok Pal

- The Constitution should be amended to provide for a national Ombudsman called the Rashtriya Lokayukta. The role and jurisdiction of the Rashtriya Lokayukta should be defined in the Constitution while the composition, mode of appointment and other details can be decided by Parliament through legislation.

- The jurisdiction of Rashtriya Lokayukta should extend to Ministers (except the Prime Minister), Chief Ministers, and Members of Parliament. In case the enquiry establishes the involvement of any other public official, it can enquire against such public servants.
- The Prime Minister should be kept out of the jurisdiction of the Rashtriya Lokayukta.
- The Rashtriya Lokayukta should consist of a serving or retired Judge of the Supreme Court as the Chairperson, an eminent jurist as Member and the Central Vigilance Commissioner as the ex-officio Member.
- The Chairperson and members of the Rashtriya Lokayukta should be selected by a Committee consisting of the Vice President, the Prime Minister, the Leader of the Opposition, the Speaker of the Lok Sabha and the Chief Justice of India. The Chairperson and Member should be appointed for only one term of three years and they should not hold any public office later, except if they can become the Chief Justice of India.

Lokayukta

- The Constitution should make it obligatory on the part of state governments to establish the institution of Lokayukta and stipulate the general principles about its structure, power and functions.
- The Lokayukta should be a multi-member body consisting of a judicial Member in the Chair, an eminent jurist or eminent administrator as Member and the head of the State Vigilance Commission as ex-officio Member.
- The Chairperson and member of the Lokayukta should be selected by a Committee of the Chief Minister, Chief Justice of the High Court and the Leader of the Opposition in

the Legislative Assembly. There is no need to have an Uplokayukta (deputy Lokayukta).

- The Chairperson and members of the Lokayukta should be appointed strictly for one term only and they should not hold any public office under government thereafter.

- The Lokayukta should have its own machinery for investigation. Initially, it may take officers on deputation from the state government, but over a period of five years, it should take steps to recruit its own cadre, and train them properly.

- All cases of corruption should be referred to Rashtriya Lokayukta or state Lokayukta and these should not be referred to any Commission of Inquiry.

- The jurisdiction of the Lokayukta would extend to only cases involving corruption. They should not look into general public grievances. The Lokayukta should deal with cases of corruption against Ministers and MLAs.

- Each State should constitute a State Vigilance Commission to look into cases of corruption against state government officials. The Commission should have three Members and have functions similar to that of the Central Vigilance Commission. The Anti Corruption Bureaus should be brought under the control of the State Vigilance Commission.

Ombudsman at Local Level

- A local bodies Ombudsman should be constituted for a group of districts to investigate cases against the functionaries of the local bodies. The State Panchayat Raj Acts and the Urban Local Bodies Act should be amended to include this provision.

- The local bodies Ombudsman should be empowered to

investigate cases of corruption or maladministration by the functionaries of the local self governments, and submit reports to the competent authorities for taking action. The competent authorities should normally take action as recommended. In case they do not agree with the recommendations, they should give their reasons in writing and the reasons should be made public.

Investigation and Prosecution

- The State Vigilance Commissions and Lokayuktas should supervise the prosecution of corruption related cases.
- The investigative agencies should acquire multi-disciplinary skills and should be thoroughly conversant with the working of various departments. Modern techniques of investigation should be used such as electronic surveillance, video and audio recording of surprise inspections, traps, searches and seizures.
- A reasonable time limit for investigation of different types of cases should be fixed for the investigative agencies.
- There should be sustained step-up in the number of cases detected and investigated. The priorities need to be reoriented by focussing on 'big' cases of corruption.
- The prosecution of corruption cases should be conducted by a panel of lawyers prepared by the Attorney General or the Advocate General in consultation with Rashtriya Lokayukta or the Lokayukta.
- The anti-corruption agencies should conduct surveys of departments with particular reference to highly corruption prone ones in order to gather intelligence and to target officers of questionable integrity.
- The economic offences unit of states needs to be strengthened to effectively investigate cases and there should be better coordination among the existing agencies.

Till 2010, 18 states have enacted laws to establish Lokayuktas. They are: Andhra Pradesh, Assam, Bihar, Chhattisgarh, Delhi, Gujarat, Jharkhand, Haryana, Himachal Pradesh, Karnataka, Kerala, Madhya Pradesh, Maharashtra, Orissa, Punjab, Rajasthan, Uttarakhand, and Uttar Pradesh.

Vohra Committee Report

The Vohra (Committee) Report was submitted by the former Indian Union Home Secretary, N.N. Vohra, in October 1993. It studied the problem of the criminalisation of politics and of the nexus among criminals, politicians and bureaucrats in India. The report contained several observations made by official agencies on the criminal network which was virtually running a parallel government. It also discussed criminal gangs who enjoyed the patronage of politicians, of all parties, and the protection of government functionaries. It revealed that political leaders had become the leaders of gangs. They were connected to the military. Over the years criminals had been elected to local bodies, State Assemblies and Parliament. The unpublished annexures to the Vohra Report were believed to contain highly explosive material. In 1997 the Supreme Court recommended the appointment of a high level committee to ensure in-depth investigation into the findings of the N.N. Vohra Committee and to secure prosecution of those involved.

[Narinder Nath Vohra is the current governor of the Indian state of Jammu and Kashmir. He took over from S.K. Sinha on June 25, 2008. He is the first civilian governor of Jammu and Kashmir in 18 years after Jagmohan.

Vohra was educated at Punjab and Oxford Universities, and served in the IAS between 1959 and 1994. He served as Principal Secretary to Prime Minister I.K. Gujral in 1997-98 and was a member of the National Security Advisory Board from

1998 to 2001 when the NDA government was in power. He also headed the National Task Force on internal security and co-chaired the India-European Union Round Table in 2001. In between, he also served as director of the India International Centre and was chairman of the IDSA review committee. For his service to the nation, Vohra was also awarded the Padma Vibhushan in 2007.

Since February 2003 until he became the governor, Vohra had been the Indian government's interlocutor in Kashmir. As such he had been holding wide-ranging discussions with both the elected representatives in the state and also the separatists in a bid to forge a common ground for the all-round development of the state. His first major action were to withdraw the controversial Amarnath shrine land transfer order.]

Citations from the report are:

- In the first meeting of the Committee (held on 15th July 1993), I had explained to the Members that Government had established the Committee after seeing the reports of our Intelligence and Investigation agencies on the activities/ linkages of the Dawood Ibrahim gang, consequent to the bomb blasts in Bombay in March 1993.

- In the bigger cities, the main source of income relates to real estate—forcibly occupying lands/buildings, procuring such properties at cheap rates by forcing out the existing occupants/tenants etc. Over time, the money power thus acquired is used for building up contacts with bureaucrats and politicians and expansion of activities with impunity. The money power is used to develop a network of muscle-power which is also used by the politicians during elections.

- "The nexus between the criminal gangs, police, bureaucracy and politicians has come out clearly in various parts of the country. The existing criminal justice system, which was essentially designed to deal with the individual offences/crimes, is unable to deal with the activities of the Mafia; the provisions of law in regard economic offences are weak (...)

- Director CBI has observed that there are many such cases, as that of [mafia boss Iqbal] MIRCHI where the initial failure has led to the emergence of Mafia giants who have become too big to be tackled.

- Like the Director CBI, the DIB has also stated that there has been a rapid spread and growth of criminal gangs, armed senas, drug Mafias, smuggling gangs, drug peddlers and economic lobbies in the country which have, over the years, developed an extensive network of contacts with the bureaucrats/Government functionaries at the local levels, politicians, media persons and strategically located individuals in the non-State sector. Some of these Syndicates also have international linkages, including the foreign intelligence agencies.

- The various crime Syndicates /Mafia organisations have developed significant muscle and money power and established linkages with governmental functionaries, political leaders and others to be able to operate with impunity.

- The various agencies presently in the field take care to essentially focus on their respective charter of duties, dealing with the infringement of laws relating to their organisations and consciously putting aside any information on linkages which they may come across.

- In the background of the discussions so far, there does not appear to be need for any further debate on the vital importance of setting up a nodal point to which all existing intelligence and Enforcement agencies (irrespective of the Department under which they are located) shall promptly pass on any information which they may come across, which relates to the activities of crime Syndicates.

Former Law Minister Ram Jethmalani, ex-Punjab DGP J.F. Ribeiro and others have filed a PIL in the SC seeking a directive to the government to bring back about $1.4 trillion allegedly held in secret bank accounts overseas by several powerful people. On 19, January 2011, it was argued in the Supreme Court that the government's failure to act on the N.N. Vohra committee recommendations for checking criminalisation of politics has led to the huge problem of black money, most of which is stashed away in Switzerland and other tax havens across the world.

Senior counsel Anil Divan, arguing for the PIL petitioners, contended that Vohra had clearly stated that the country would find itself in a dismal state unless the government came down heavily on such unscrupulous elements. In view of the sensitive nature of the issue, Vohra himself had taken the trouble of drafting and finalising the report and had gone on record stating that even the committee members were apprehensive about expressing their views.

Among other things, the committee had suggested putting in place legal provisions for attaching the property of mafia elements. But the government had done nothing to attach the property of one Hassan Ali Khan, a Pune-based businessman, found to be holding as much as $8 billion in a foreign bank though he had declared an annual income of just Rs.15 lakh to the income tax authorities. Investigations had shown that he had received funds from international arms smuggler Adnan Khashoggi, Divan said.

Solicitor General Gopal Subramanium said the Centre had

set up the National Investigation Agency (NIA) after the November 2008 Mumbai terror attack only on the recommendations of the committee.

Right to Information (RTI) Act

Disclosure of State information in British India was (and is) governed from 1889 by the Official Secrets Act. This law secures information related to security of the State, sovereignty of the country and friendly relations with foreign states, and contains provisions which prohibit disclosure of non-classified information. Civil Service conduct rules and the Indian Evidence Act impose further restrictions on government officials' powers to disclose information to the public.

Passage of a national level law, however, proved to be a difficult task. Given the experience of state governments in passing practicable legislation, the Central Government appointed a working group under H.D. Shourie and assigned it the task of drafting legislation. The Shourie draft, in an extremely diluted form, was the basis for the Freedom of Information Bill, 2000 which eventually became law under the Freedom of Information Act, 2002. This Act was severely criticised for permitting too many exemptions, not only under the standard grounds of national security and sovereignty, but also for requests that would involve "disproportionate diversion of the resources of a public authority". There was no upper limit on the charges that could be levied. There were no penalties for not complying with a request for information. The FoI Act, consequently, never came into effective force.

The doomed FoI Act led to sustained pressure for a better National RTI enactment. The first draft of the Right to Information Bill was presented to Parliament on 22 December 2004. After intense debate, more than a hundred amendments to the draft Bill were made between December 2004 and 15 June 2005, when the bill finally passed. The Act came fully into effect on 13 October 2005.

The RTI Laws were first successfully enacted by the state governments of—Tamil Nadu (1997), Goa (1997), Rajasthan (2000), Karnataka (2000), Delhi (2001), Maharashtra (2002), Assam (2002), Madhya Pradesh (2003), and Jammu and Kashmir (2004). The Maharashtra and Delhi State level enactments are considered to have been the most widely used. The Delhi RTI Act is still in force. Jammu & Kashmir, has its own Right to Information Act of 2009, the successor to the repealed J&K Right to Information Act, 2004 and its 2008 amendment.

The Act covers the whole of India except Jammu and Kashmir, where J&K Right to Information Act is in force. It is applicable to all constitutional authorities, including the executive, legislature and judiciary; any institution or body established or constituted by an act of Parliament or a state legislature. It is also defined in the Act that bodies or authorities established or constituted by order or notification of appropriate government including bodies "owned, controlled or substantially financed" by government, or non-Government organisations "substantially financed, directly or indirectly by funds" provided by the government are also covered in it.

Under the Act, all authorities covered must appoint their Public Information Officer (PIO). Any person may submit a request to the PIO for information in writing. It is the PIO's obligation to provide information to citizens of India who request information under the Act. If the request pertains to another public authority (in whole or part) it is the PIO's responsibility to transfer/forward the concerned portions of the request to a PIO of the other within 5 days. In addition, every public authority is required to designate Assistant Public Information Officers (APIOs) to receive RTI requests and appeals for forwarding to the PIOs of their public authority. The applicant is not required to disclose any information or reasons other than his name and contact particulars to seek the information.

The Act specifies time limits for replying to the request.

- If the request has been made to the PIO, the reply is to be given within 30 days of receipt.
- If the request has been made to an APIO, the reply is to be given within 35 days of receipt.
- If the PIO transfers the request to another public authority (better concerned with the information requested), the time allowed to reply is 30 days but computed from the day after it is received by the PIO of the transferee authority.
- Information concerning corruption and Human Rights violations by scheduled Security agencies (those listed in the Second Schedule to the Act) is to be provided within 45 days but with the prior approval of the Central Information Commission.
- However, if life or liberty of any person is involved, the PIO is expected to reply within 48 hours.

Since the information is to be paid for, the reply of the PIO is necessarily limited to either denying the request (in whole or part) and/or providing a computation of "further fees". The time between the reply of the PIO and the time taken to deposit the further fees for information is excluded from the time allowed. If information is not provided within this period, it is treated as deemed refusal. Refusal with or without reasons may be ground for appeal or complaint. Further, information not provided in the times prescribed is to be provided free of charge.

For Central Departments as of 2006, there is a fee of Rs. 10 for filing the request, Rs. 2 per page of information and Rs. 5 for each hour of inspection after the first hour. If the applicant is a Below Poverty Card holder, then no fee shall apply. Such BPL Card holders have to provide a copy of their BPL card along with their application to the Public Authority. States Government and High Courts fix their own rules.

Central Intelligence and Security agencies are specified in the Second Schedule like IB, RAW, Central Bureau of Investigation (CBI), Directorate of Revenue Intelligence, Central Economic Intelligence Bureau, Directorate of Enforcement, Narcotics Control Bureau, Aviation Research Centre, Special Frontier Force, BSF, CRPF, ITBP, CISF, NSG, Assam Rifles, Special Service Bureau, Special Branch (CID), Andaman and Nicobar, The Crime Branch-CID-CB, Dadra and Nagar Haveli and Special Branch, Lakshadweep Police. Agencies specified by the State Governments through a Notification will also be excluded. The exclusion, however, is not absolute and these organisations have an obligation to provide information pertaining to allegations of corruption and human rights violations. Further, information relating to allegations of human rights violation could be given but only with the approval of the Central or State Information Commission.

The following is exempt from disclosure [S.8)]

- Information, disclosure of which would prejudicially affect the sovereignty and integrity of India, the security, "strategic, scientific or economic" interests of the State, relation with foreign State or lead to incitement of an offense;

- Information which has been expressly forbidden to be published by any court of law or tribunal or the disclosure of which may constitute contempt of court;

- Information, the disclosure of which would cause a breach of privilege of Parliament or the State Legislature;
- Information including commercial confidence, trade secrets or intellectual property, the disclosure of which would harm the competitive position of a third party, unless the competent authority is satisfied that larger public interest warrants the disclosure of such information;
- Information available to a person in his fiduciary relationship, unless the competent authority is satisfied that the larger public interest warrants the disclosure of such information;
- Information received in confidence from foreign Government;
- Information, the disclosure of which would endanger the life or physical safety of any person or identify the source of information or assistance given in confidence for law enforcement or security purposes;
- Information which would impede the process of investigation or apprehension or prosecution of offenders;
- Cabinet papers including records of deliberations of the Council of Ministers, Secretaries and other officers;
- Information which relates to personal information the disclosure of which has no relationship to any public activity or interest, or which would cause unwarranted invasion of the privacy of the individual (but it is also provided that the information which cannot be denied to the Parliament or a State Legislature shall not be denied by this exemption);
- Notwithstanding any of the exemptions listed above, a public authority may allow access to information, if public interest in disclosure outweighs the harm to the protected interests. [NB: This provision is qualified by the proviso

to sub-section 11(1) of the Act which exempts disclosure of "trade or commercial secrets protected by law" under this clause when read along with 8(1)(d)].

Deficiencies in the Present Anti-corruption Systems

At central Government level, there is Central Vigilance Commission, Departmental vigilance and CBI. CVC and Departmental vigilance deal with vigilance (disciplinary proceedings) aspect of a corruption case and CBI deals with criminal aspect of that case.

Central Vigilance Commission (CVC)

- CVC is the apex body for all vigilance cases in Government of India.

- However, it does not have adequate resources commensurate with the large number of complaints that it receives. CVC is a very small set up with staff strength less than 200. It is supposed to check corruption in more than 1500 central government departments and ministries, some of them being as big as Central Excise, Railways, Income Tax etc. Therefore, it has to depend on the vigilance wings of respective departments and forwards most of the complaints for inquiry and report to them. While it monitors the progress of these complaints, there is delay and the complainants are often disturbed by this. It directly enquires into a few complaints on its own, especially when it suspects motivated delays or where senior officials could be implicated. But given the constraints of manpower, such number is really small.

- CVC is merely an advisory body. Central Government Departments seek CVC's advice on various corruption cases. However, they are free to accept or reject CVC's advice. Even in those cases, which are directly enquired into by the CVC, it can only advise government. CVC mentions these cases of non-acceptance in its monthly reports and the Annual Report to Parliament. But these are not much in focus in Parliamentary debates or by the media.

- Experience shows that CVC's advice to initiate prosecution is rarely accepted and whenever CVC advised major penalty, it was reduced to minor penalty. Therefore, CVC can hardly be treated as an effective deterrent against corruption.

- CVC cannot direct CBI to initiate enquiries against any officer of the level of Joint Secretary and above on its own. The CBI has to seek the permission of that department, which obviously would not be granted if the senior officers of that department are involved and they could delay the case or see to it that permission would not be granted.

- CVC does not have powers to register criminal case. It deals only with vigilance or disciplinary matters.

- It does not have powers over politicians. If there is an involvement of a politician in any case, CVC could at best bring it to the notice of the Government. There are several cases of serious corruption in which officials and political executive are involved together.

- It does not have any direct powers over departmental vigilance wings. Often it is seen that CVC forwards a complaint to a department and then keeps sending reminders to them to enquire and send report. Many a times, the departments just do not comply. CVC does not have any really effective powers over them to seek compliance of its orders.

- CVC does not have administrative control over officials in vigilance wings of various central government departments to which it forwards corruption complaints. Though the government does consult CVC before appointing the Chief

Vigilance Officers of various departments, however, the final decision lies with the government. Also, the officials below CVO are appointed/transferred by that department only. Only in exceptional cases, if the CVO chooses to bring it to the notice of CVC, CVC could bring pressure on the Department to revoke orders but again such recommendations are not binding.

- Appointments to CVC are directly under the control of ruling political party, though the leader of the Opposition is a member of the Committee to select CVC and VCs. But the Committee only considers names put up before it and that is decided by the Government. The appointments are opaque.

- CVC Act gives supervisory powers to CVC over CBI. However, these supervisory powers have remained ineffective. CVC does not have the power to call for any file from CBI or to direct them to do any case in a particular manner. Besides, CBI is under administrative control of DOPT rather than CVC.

Therefore, though CVC is relatively independent in its functioning it neither has resources nor powers to enquire and take action on complaints of corruption in a manner that meets the expectations of people or act as an effective deterrence against corruption.

Departmental Vigilance Wings

- Each Department has a vigilance wing, which is manned by officials from the same department (barring a few which have an outsider as Chief Vigilance Officer. However, all the officers under him belong to the same department).

- Since the officers in the vigilance wing of a department are from the same department and they can be posted to any position in that department any time, it is practically impossible for them to be independent and objective while inquiring into complaints against their colleagues and seniors. If a complaint is received against a senior officer, it is impossible to enquire into that complaint because an officer who is in vigilance today might get posted under that senior officer some time in future.

- In some departments, especially in the Ministries, some officials double up as vigilance officials. It means that an existing official is given additional duty of vigilance also. So, if some citizen complaints against that officer, the complaints expected to be enquired into by the same officer. Even if someone complaints against that officer to the CVC or to the Head of that Department or to any other authority, the complaint is forwarded by all these agencies and it finally lands up in his own lap to enquire against himself. Even if he recuses himself from such inquiries , still they have to be handled by those who otherwise report to him. There are indeed examples of such absurdity.

- There have been instances of the officials posted in vigilance wing by that department having had a very corrupt past. While in vigilance, they try to scuttle all cases against themselves. They also turn vigilance wing into a hub of corruption, where cases are closed for consideration.

- Departmental vigilance does not investigate into criminal aspect of any case. It does not have the powers to register an FIR.

- They also do not have any powers against politicians.

Since the vigilance wing is directly under the control of the Head of that Department, it is practically impossible for them to enquire against senior officials of that department. Therefore, the vigilance wing of any department is seen to soft pedal on genuine complaints or used to enquire against "inconvenient" officers.

Central Bureau of Investigation (CBI)

- CBI has powers of a police station to investigate and register FIR. It can investigate any case related to a Central Government department on its own or any case referred to it by any state government or any court.
- CBI is overburdened and does not accept cases even where amount of defalcation is alleged to be around Rs 1 crore.
- CBI is directly under the administrative control of Central Government.
- So, if a complaint pertains to any minister or politician who is part of a ruling coalition or a bureaucrat who is close to them, CBI's credibility has suffered and there is increasing public perception that it cannot do a fair investigation and that it is influenced to scuttle these cases.
- Again, because CBI is directly under the control of Central Government, CBI is perceived to have been often used to settle scores against in convenient politicians.

Therefore, if a citizen wants to make a complaint about corruption by a politician or an official in the Central Government, there isn't a single anti-corruption agency which is effective and independent of the government, whose wrongdoings are sought to be investigated. CBI has powers but it is not independent. CVC is independent but it does not have sufficient powers or resources.

The Fallout

It has also helped activists uncover graft cases against various politicians and bureaucrats. To quell the findings made by RTI activists, there have been instances where RTI activists have been attacked and even killed in some cases. In the first year of National RTI, 42,876 (not yet official) applications for information were filed to Central (i.e. Federal) public authorities. Of these 878 were disputed at the final appellate stage—the Central Information Commission at New Delhi. A few of these decisions have thereafter been mired in further legal controversy in the various High Courts of India. The first stay order against a final appellate decision of the Central Information Commission was granted on 3 May 2006 by the High Court of Delhi. The Government of India's purported intention in 2006 to amend the RTI Act was postponed after public disquiet, but has been revived again in 2009.

According to PRS Legislative Research:

- Prosecution of public servants for corruption may usually be taken up only after the respective government gives sanction to do so. This provision is designed to protect honest officials from harassment. However, the provision may be misused by delaying response to requests for sanction. As of end-2010, the central government had not provided responses to 236 requests. Of these, 155 requests (66%) were pending for over three months. State governments had not responded to 84 requests, of which 13 (15%) were pending for more than three months.
- "The Central Vigilance Commission (CVC) is the premier agency tasked to tackle corruption cases within the central government. Between 2005 and 2009, penalties were imposed on 13,061 cases (average 2612 per year) based on the CVC's advice. This included 846 cases (annual average 169), in which sanction was granted for criminal prosecution. Major penalties were imposed in 4895 cases (annual average 979). These include dismissal, reduction to lower rank, cut in pension etc.

Minor penalties such as censure were imposed on 5356 cases (annual average 1071), and administrative action was taken in 1964 cases (annual average 393).

- The Central Bureau of Investigation (CBI) is the main agency used by the CVC to investigate cases of corruption and misuse of office by public officials. As of December 2010, 21 percent of the sanctioned posts in CBI were vacant. This includes 52 percent of the posts of law officers, 65 percent of technical officers and 21 percent of executive officers.

- The criminal justice system has also been slow in prosecuting the CBI cases. As of end-2010, there were 9,927 CBI cases pending in courts. Of these, 2,245 cases (23 percent of the total) were pending for more than 10 years.

- After the murder of Satyendra Dubey, the Supreme Court directed the government in 2004 to put a mechanism to act on complaints from whistle-blowers. In April 2004, the government passed a resolution to empower the CVC to act on complaints from whistleblowers. In the five years from 2005 to 2009, the CVC received a total of 1,731 complaints, or an annual average of 346. The government has introduced the Public Interest Disclosure Bill, 2010, which is currently being examined by the Parliamentary Standing Committee.

In the period 2010-11, India witnessed various scandals being blown apart by the media, whistle-blowers, civil society activists and government investigation agencies alike. Scams like 2G spectrum scam, Adarsh Housing Society Scam, Commonwealth Games scam and many more brought about name of various Cabinet Ministers, Chief Ministers and even members of the Armed Forces. This showed how deeply corruption entrenched has become in India. It has led to a more expansive civil society movement that wishes to fight graft with the strictest of laws and penalties.

Critique of the Government Lokpal Bill

As Hazare told reporters in New Delhi, the Lokpal Bill has been introduced in Parliament eight times in the past four decades, the first time in 1969. But, it has never been passed apparently because politicians do not want to be held accountable.

The India Against Corruption group said it regrets that the latest draft of the Lokpal Bill prepared by the current UPA government demolishes whatever little exists in the name of the anti-corruption mechanism in the country and seeks to insulate politicians from action. This, its members say, is the reason why it has come out with another version of the Bill. The group argues that the Lokayukta Acts enacted by 18 states have proved to be quite ineffective.

On its website *indiaagainstcorruption.org*, the group presents a critique of the government Bill and gives 17 reasons why it is eyewash. Here are some of the points raised by Hazare's group:

1. *Government's proposal:* Lokpal will not have any power to either initiate action suo motu in any case or even receive complaints of corruption from general public. The general public will make complaints to the speaker of Lok Sabha or chairperson of Rajya Sabha. Only those complaints forwarded by Speaker of Lok Sabha/Chairperson of Rajya Sabha to Lokpal would be investigated by Lokpal. This not only severely restricts the functioning of Lokpal, it also provides a tool in the hands of the ruling party to have only those cases referred to Lokpal which pertain to political opponents (since speaker is always from the ruling party).

It will also provide a tool in the hands of the ruling party to protect its own politicians.

Civil Society proposal: Lokpal will have powers to initiate investigations *suo moto* in any case and also to directly entertain complaints from the public. It will not need reference or permission from anyone to initiate investigation into any case.

2. *Government's proposal:* Lokpal has been proposed to be an advisory body. Lokpal, after enquiry in any case, will forward its report to the competent authority. The competent authority will have final powers to decide whether to take action on Lokpa's report or not. In the case of cabinet ministers the competent authority is Prime Minister. In the case of PM and MPs the competent authority is Lok Sabha or Rajya Sabha, as the case may be. In the coalition era when the government of the day depends upon the support of its political partners, it will be impossible for the PM to act against any of his cabinet ministers on the basis of Lokpal's report. For instance, if there were such a Lokpal today and if Lokpal made a recommendation to the PM to prosecute A. Raja, obviously the PM will not have the political courage to initiate prosecution against A. Raja. Likewise, if Lokpal made a report against the PM or any MP of the ruling party, will the house ever pass a resolution to prosecute the PM or the ruling party MP? Obviously, they will never do that.

Civil Society proposal: Lokpal is not an advisory body. It will have the powers to initiate prosecution against any one after completion of investigations in any case. It will also have powers to order disciplinary proceedings against any government servant

3. *Government's proposal:* The bill is legally unsound. Lokpal has

not been given police powers. Therefore Lokpal cannot register an FIR. Therefore all the enquiries conducted by Lokpal will tantamount to preliminary enquiries. Even if the report of Lokpal is accepted, who will file the charge sheet in the court? Who will initiate prosecution? Who will appoint the prosecution lawyer? The entire bill is silent on that.

Civil Society Proposal: Lokpal would have police powers. It will be able to register FIR, proceed with criminal investigations and launch prosecution.

4. *Government's proposal:* The bill does not say what will be the role of CBI after this bill. Can CBI and Lokpal investigate the same case or CBI will lose its powers to investigate politicians? If the latter is true, then this bill is meant to completely insulate politicians from any investigations whatsoever which are possible today through CBI.

Civil Society proposal: That part of CBI, which deals with cases of corruption, will be merged into Lokpal so that there is just one effective and independent body to take action against corruption.

5. *Government's proposal:* There is a strong punishment for frivolous complaints. If any complaint is found to be false and frivolous, Lokpal will have the power to send the complainant to jail through summary trial but if the complaint were found to be true, the Lokpal will not have the power to send the corrupt politicians to jail! So the bill appears to be meant to browbeat, threaten and discourage those fighting against corruption.

Civil Society proposal: Deterrence has been provided against frivolous complaints in the form of financial penalties against the complainant, however, Lokayukta is empowered to prosecute the corrupt and take disciplinary action against them.

6. *Government's proposal:* Lokpal will have jurisdiction only on MPs, ministers and PM. It will not have jurisdiction over officers. The officers and politicians do not indulge in corruption separately. In any case of corruption, there is always an involvement of both of them. So according to government's proposal, every case would need to be investigated by both CVC and Lokpal. So now, in each case, CVC will look into the role of bureaucrats while Lokpal will look into the role of politicians. Obviously the case records will be with one agency and the way government functions it will not share its records with the other agency. It is also possible that in the same case the two agencies arrive at completely opposite conclusions. Therefore it appears to be a sure way of killing any case.

Civil Society proposal: Lokpal will have jurisdiction over politicians, officials and judges. CVC and the entire vigilance machinery of government will be merged into Lokpal.

7. *Government's proposal:* Lokpal will consist of three members, all of them being retired judges. There is no reason why the choice should be restricted to judiciary. By creating so many post-retirement posts for judges, the government will make the retiring judges vulnerable to government influences just before retirement as is already happening in the case of retiring bureaucrats. The retiring judges, in the hope of getting post retirement employment would do the bidding of the government in their last few years.

Civil Society proposal: Lokpal would have ten members and one Chairperson. Out of them four need to have legal background (they need not be judges). Others could be from any background.

8. *Government's proposal:* The selection committee consists of Vice President, PM, Leaders of both houses, Leaders of

opposition in both houses, Law Minister and Home minister. Barring Vice President, all of them are politicians whose corruption Lokpal is supposed to investigate. So there is a direct conflict of interest. Also selection committee is heavily loaded in favour of the ruling party. Effectively ruling party will make the final selections. And obviously ruling party will never appoint strong and effective Lokpal.

Civil Society proposal: Selection committee consists of members from judicial background, Chief Election Commissioner, Comptroller and Auditor General of India and international awardees (like Nobel Prize winners and Magsaysay awardees of Indian origin). A detailed transparent and participatory selection process has been prescribed.

9. *Government's proposal:* Lokpal will not have powers to investigate any case against PM, which deals with foreign affairs, security and defence. This means that corruption in defence deals will be out of any scrutiny whatsoever. It will become impossible to investigate into any Bofors in future.
   Civil Society proposal: There is no such bar on Lokpal's powers.

10. *Government's proposal:* Whereas a time limit of six months to one year has been prescribed for Lokpal to enquire, however, subsequently, there is no time limit prescribed for completion of trial.
    Civil Society proposal: Investigations should be completed within one year. Trial should get over within the next one year.

11. *Government's proposal:* It does not deal with corruption of Bureaucrats. Corrupt bureaucrats continue in their job without any actions against them.

Civil Society proposal: Lokpal will have power to direct disciplinary action, including dismissal of a corrupt officer from job

12. *Government's proposal:* It does not talk of investigation of complaints against judges
    Civil Society proposal: Lokpal will have powers to initiate investigations on complaints of corruption against judges.

13. *Government's proposal:* Speaker would decide which complaints shall be enquired into by Lokpal.
    Civil Society proposal: Lokpal will not be able to dismiss any complaint from public without hearing the complainant.

14. *Government's proposal:* Our entire governance system suffers from inadequate public grievance redressal systems, which force people to pay bribes. Lokpal bill does not address this issue.
    Civil Society proposal: Lokpal will have the powers to orders redressal in a time bound manner. It will have powers to impose financial penalties on guilty officers, which would be paid to complainant as compensation.

15. *Government's proposal:* Large numbers of people raising their voices against political corruption are being murdered. Lokpal does not have any powers to provide protection to them.
    Civil Society proposal: Lokpal will have powers to provide protection against physical and professional victimisation of whistleblowers.

16. *Government's proposal:* Nothing has been provided in law to recover ill gotten wealth. A corrupt person can come out of jail and enjoy that money.
    Civil Society proposal: Loss caused to the government due to corruption will be recovered from all accused.

17. *Government's proposal:* Under the present law, there is small punishment for corruption—Punishment for corruption is minimum 6 months and maximum 7 years.
Civil Society proposal: Enhanced punishment—The punishment would be minimum 5 years and maximum of life imprisonment.

Jan Lokpal Bill: The Alternative

The Jan Lokpal Bill (Citizen's ombudsman Bill) is a draft anti-corruption bill drawn up by prominent civil society activists seeking the appointment of a Jan Lokpal, an independent body that would investigate corruption cases, complete the investigation within a year and envisages trial in the case getting over in the next one year.

Drafted by Justice Santosh Hegde (former Supreme Court Judge and present Lokayukta of Karnataka), Prashant Bhushan (Supreme Court Lawyer) and Arvind Kejriwal (RTI activist), the draft Bill envisages a system where a corrupt person found guilty would go to jail within two years of the complaint being made and his ill-gotten wealth being confiscated. It also seeks power to the Jan Lokpal to prosecute politicians and bureaucrats without government permission.

Retired IPS officer Kiran Bedi and other known people like Swami Agnivesh, Sri Sri Ravi Shankar, Anna Hazare and Mallika Sarabhai are also part of the movement, called India Against Corruption. Its website describes the movement as "an expression of collective anger of people of India against corruption. We have all come together to force/request/persuade/pressurize the Government to enact the Jan Lokpal Bill. We feel that if this Bill were enacted it would create an effective deterrence against corruption."

A look at the salient features of Jan Lokpal Bill:

1. An institution called LOKPAL at the centre and Lokayukta in each state will be set up.

2. Like Supreme Court and Election Commission, they will be completely independent of the governments. No minister or bureaucrat will be able to influence their investigations.

3. Cases against corrupt people will not linger on for years any more: Investigations in any case will have to be completed in one year. Trial should be completed in next one year so that the corrupt politician, officer or judge is sent to jail within two years.

4. The loss that a corrupt person caused to the government will be recovered at the time of conviction.

5. How will it help a common citizen: If any work of any citizen is not done in prescribed time in any government office, Lokpal will impose financial penalty on guilty officers, which will be given as compensation to the complainant.

6. So, you could approach Lokpal if your ration card or passport or voter card is not being made or if police is not registering your case or any other work is not being done in prescribed time. Lokpal will have to get it done in a month's time. You could also report any case of corruption to Lokpal like ration being siphoned off, poor quality roads been constructed or panchayat funds being siphoned off. Lokpal will have to complete its investigations in a year, trial will be over in next one year and the guilty will go to jail within two years.

7. But won't the government appoint corrupt and weak people as Lokpal members? That won't be possible because

its members will be selected by judges, citizens and constitutional authorities and not by politicians, through a completely transparent and participatory process.

8. What if some officer in Lokpal becomes corrupt? The entire functioning of Lokpal/ Lokayukta will be completely transparent. Any complaint against any officer of Lokpal shall be investigated and the officer dismissed within two months.

9. What will happen to existing anti-corruption agencies? CVC, departmental vigilance and anti-corruption branch of CBI will be merged into Lokpal. Lokpal will have complete powers and machinery to independently investigate and prosecute any officer, judge or politician.

10. It will be the duty of the Lokpal to provide protection to those who are being victimised for raising their voice against corruption.

Letter to Prime Minister

Anna Hazare takes the Prime Minister to task in his five-point letter, explaining once again why exactly he is on an indefinite fast at Jantar Mantar. The letter as follows:

Dear Dr. Singh,

I have started my indefinite fast at Jantar Mantar. I had invited you also to fast and pray for a corruption free India on 5th April. Though I did not receive any reply from you, I am hopeful that you must have done that.

I am pained to read and hear about government's reaction to my fast. I consider it my duty to clarify the points raised on behalf of Congress party and the government by their spokespersons, as they appear in media:

1. It is being alleged that I am being instigated by some people

to sit on this fast. Dear Manmohan Singh ji, this is an insult to my sense of wisdom and intelligence. I am not a kid that I could be "instigated" into going on an indefinite fast. I am a fiercely independent person. I take advice from many friends and critics, but do what my conscience directs me to do. It is my experience that when cornered, governments resort to such malicious slandering. I am pained that the government, rather than addressing the issue of corruption, is trying to allege conspiracies, when there are none.

2. It is being said that I have shown impatience. Dear Prime Minister, so far, every government has shown complete insensitivity and lack of political commitment to tackling corruption. 62 years after independence, we still do not have independent and effective anti-corruption systems. Very weak versions of Lokpal Bill were presented in Parliament eight times in last 42 years. Even these weak versions were not passed by Parliament. This means, left to themselves, the politicians and bureaucrats will never pass any law which subjects them to any kind of objective scrutiny. At a time, when the country has witnessed scams of unprecedented scale, the impatience of the entire country is justified. And we call upon you, not to look for precedents, but show courage to take unprecedented steps.

3. It is being said that I have shown impatience when the government has "initiated" the process. I would urge you to tell me—exactly what processes are underway?

   a. You say that your Group of Ministers are drafting the anti-corruption law. Many of the members of this Group of Ministers have such a shady past that if effective anti-corruption systems had been in place, some of them would have been behind bars. Do you want us to have faith in a process in which some of the most corrupt people of this country should draft the anti corruption law?

b. NAC subcommittee has discussed Jan Lokpal Bill. But what does that actually mean? Will the government accept the recommendations of NAC sub-committee? So far, UPA II has shown complete contempt for even the most innocuous issues raised by NAC.

c. I and many other friends from India Against Corruption movement wrote several letters to you after 1st December. I also sent you a copy of Jan Lokpal Bill on 1st December. We did not get any response. It is only when I wrote to you that I will sit on an indefinite fast, we were promptly invited for discussions on 7th March. I wonder whether the government responds only to threats of indefinite fast. Before that, representatives of India Against Corruption had been meeting various Ministers seeking their support for the Jan Lokpal Bill. They met Mr Moily also and personally handed over copy of Jan Lokpal to him. A few hours before our meeting with you, we received a phone call from Mr Moily's office that the copy of Jan Lokpal Bill had been misplaced by his office and they wanted another copy. This is the seriousness with which the government has dealt with Jan Lokpal Bill.

d. Dear Dr Manmohan Singh ji, if you were in my place, would you have any faith in the aforesaid processes? Kindly let me know if there are any other processes underway. If you still feel that I am impatient, I am happy that I am because the whole nation is feeling impatient at the lack of credible efforts from your government against corruption.

4. What are we asking for? We are not saying that you should accept the Bill drafted by us. But kindly create a credible platform for discussions—a joint committee with at least

half members from civil society suggested by us. Your spokespersons are misleading the nation when they say that there is no precedent for setting up a joint committee. At least seven laws in Maharashtra were drafted by similar joint committees and presented in Maharashtra Assembly. Maharashtra RTI Act, one of the best laws of those times, was drafted by a joint committee. Even at the centre, when 25,000 tribals came to Delhi two years ago, your government set up a joint committee on land issues within 48 hours. You yourself are the Chairperson of that committee.

This means that the government is willing to set up joint committees on all other issues, but not on corruption. Why?

5. It is being said that the government wants to talk to us and we are not talking to them. This is utterly false. Tell me a single meeting when you called us and we did not come. We strongly believe in dialogue and engagement. Kindly do not mislead the country by saying that we are shunning dialogue.

We request you to take some credible steps at stemming corruption. Kindly stop finding faults and suspecting conspiracies in our movement. There are none. Even if there were, it does not absolve you of your responsibilities to stop corruption.

With warm regards,

K B Hazare

CHAPTER 4

Anna Hazare: A Life in Action

Early Life

Kisan Bapat Baburao Hazare, known as Anna Hazare was born on 15 January 1940 in a small village, Bhingar, near Ahmednagar city in India. There is a legend that Bhringu rishi did tapsya here on a hillock where a temple is erected in his honour. The name Bhingar is derived from the sage. Anna's father Baburao Hazare worked as an unskilled labourer in Ayurveda Ashram Pharmacy. Anna's grandfather was in the army and was posted at Bhingar when Anna was born. He died in 1945 but Anna's father continued to stay at Bhingar.

In 1952 Anna's father resigned from his job and returned to his own village, Ralegan Siddhi. At that time Anna had completed his education upto 4th standard and had six younger siblings. It was with great difficulty that Anna's father could make two ends meet. Anna's aunt (father's sister) took Anna to Mumbai. She was childless and she offered to look after him and his education.

Anna studied upto the 7th standard in Mumbai. He took up a job after the 7th standard in consideration of the economic situation back home. Anna's father at Ralegan had to work as a daily wage labourer and found it difficult to sustain his family. He was slipping deeper and deeper into debt. He had to sell off one part of his land and mortgage the other. Anna started selling flowers at Dadar in order to make his living. But Anna's working at somebody's shop for Rs. 40 a month was not enough. After gaining some experience, he started his own shop and even brought two of his brothers to Mumbai. Gradually Anna's income went up to Rs. 700 to 800 per month.

In the Indian Army

Anna Hazare started his career as a driver in the Indian Army. He spent his spare time reading the books of Swami Vivekananda, Mahatma Gandhi and Acharya Vinoba Bhave. In the year 1965, Pakistan attacked India and at that time, Hazare was posted at the Khemkaran border. On November 12, 1965, Pakistan launched air attacks on Indian base and all of Hazare's comrades became martyrs. It was a close shave for Hazare as one bullet had passed by his head.

According to his official biography, Hazare believes this was the turning point of his life as it meant he had a purpose to life. Anna was greatly influenced by Swami Vivekananda's teachings. It was at that particular moment that Hazare took an oath to dedicate his life in the service of humanity, at the age of 26. He decided not to let go of a life time by being involved merely in earning the daily bread for the family. That's the reason why he pledged to be a bachelor. By then he had completed only three years in the army and so would not be eligible for the pension scheme. In order to be self-sufficient, he continued to be in the army for 12 more years.

In Ralegan Siddhi

After voluntary retirement from the army, Hazare came to Ralegan Siddhi village in 1975.

While in the army, he used to visit his village for two months, every year during his leave period. The condition of the village was pathetic and awful. The land was barren and undulated. As the village is located in the rain-shadow area, the annual rainfall is a meager 400–500 mm. All of the rainwater use to run off and get wasted. There were no means to harvest this precious resource. Whatever rainwater use to get collected was sufficient to cultivate only one crop on 300–350 acres of land out of a total 2200 acres of land available in village. 80 percent families were surviving on one square meal in a day.

As food production was insufficient and no employment opportunities were available in the village, some villagers started brewing liquor to earn their livelihood. Gradually the number of breweries rose to 35. They were aware that what they were doing was socially and morally incorrect, but the circumstances forced them to adopt this profession for their livelihood. Some villagers had to walk 5-6 km. each day in search of employment in the nearby villages.

The helplessness due to poverty and indebtedness led people to desperation and ultimately to alcoholism. Quarrels and street fights became daily chores. Hazare's house was in a hamlet just half a km. away from the centre of the village. Hazare avoided going to the heart of the village due to this pathetic condition. He always felt helpless since he could not do anything to change the conditions prevailing in the village.

Initially, he organised the youth of the village into an organisation named the Tarun Mandal (Youth Association). He also helped to form the Pani Puravatha Mandals (Water Supply Associations) to ensure proper distribution of water.

Uprooting Alcoholism

As the next step towards social and economic change, Anna Hazare and the youth group decided to take up the issue of Alcoholism. It was very clear that there could be no progress and happiness in the village unless the curse of alcoholism was completely removed from their lives. At a meeting conducted in the temple, the villagers resolved to close down the liquor dens and ban the drinking of alcohol in the village. Since these resolutions were made in the temple, they became in a sense religious commitments. Over thirty liquor brewing units were closed by their owners voluntarily. Those who did not succumb to social pressure were forced to close down their businesses, when the youth group smashed up their liquor dens. The owners could not complain as their business was illegal.

Though the closure of liquor brewing reduced alcoholism in Ralegan Siddhi, some villagers continued to drink; they obtained their liquor from neighbouring villages. The villagers decided that those men would be given three warnings, after which they would be physically punished. Twelve men who were found in a drunken state even after initial warnings were tied to a pole with help from the youth group and flogged.

Anna Hazare appealed to the government of Maharashtra to bring in a law whereby prohibition would come into force in a village if 25 percent of the women in the village demanded it. He says, "Doesn't a mother administer bitter medicines to a sick child when she knows that the medicine can cure her child? The child may not like the medicine, but the mother does it only because she cares for the child. The alcoholics were punished so that their families would not be destroyed."

In July 2009, the state government issued a government resolution amending the Bombay Prohibition Act, 1949. As per the amendments, if at least 25 percent of women voters demand liquor prohibition through a written application to the state excise department, voting should be conducted through a secret ballot. If 50 percent of the voters vote against the sale of liquor prohibition should be imposed in the village and the sale of liquor should be stopped. Similar action can be taken at the ward level in municipal areas. Thereafter, another circular was issued, making it mandatory to get the sanction of gram the sabha for issuing new permits for sale of liquor. In some instances, when women agitated against the sale of liquor, cases were filed against them. Anna took up the issue again and in August 2009 the government issued another circular that sought withdrawal of cases against women who sought prohibition of liquor in their villages.

Along with the removal of alcohol from the village, it was decided to ban the sale of tobacco, cigarettes and beedies. In order to implement this resolution, the youth group performed a unique "Holi" twenty two years ago. The festival of Holi is celebrated as symbolic burning of evil. The youth group brought all the tobacco, cigarettes and beedies from the shops in the village and burnt them in 'Holi' fire. From that day, no tobacco, cigarettes, or beedies are sold in any shop at Ralegan Siddhi. Today there is not a single shop in Ralegaon Siddhi selling cigarettes or bidis.

The Watershed Development Programme

When he decided to dedicate his life for social cause in 1975, he believed charity should begin from home. Swami Vivekananda's words resonated in his mind—people would not listen to philosophical ideologies with empty stomachs. Social change is not possible if people are haunted by the daily problem of making two ends meet. Hazare taxed his brains on how to solve this crucial problem. He motivated the residents of the village into 'shramdan' (voluntary labour) to build canals, small-scale check-dams and percolation tanks in the nearby hills for watershed development; efforts that solved the problem of scarcity of water in the village that also made irrigation possible. The first embankment that was built using volunteer efforts developed a leak and had to be reconstructed this time with government funding.

According to the official website, he remembered that Late Mr. Vilasrao Salunkhe had in 1972, started experiments in watershed development and water management in some villages near Saswad in Pune district. His work used to be frequently discussed in informal gatherings everywhere. So, Hazare visited his project and was inspired. He then paid a visit to the office of the then Director of Agriculture, and told him that he had decided to work for betterment of his fellow villagers. He expressed his desire to undertake water conservation work in his village under his guidance. After some days, Director of Agriculture paid a visit to Ralegan Siddhi along with his subordinates and made a geographical survey. He was convinced that the topography of the village was suitable for undertaking the watershed development programme and took a decision to implement it. So far, 48 nulla bunds, 5 cement check dams and 16 Gabion structures have been constructed.

Hazare also took steps to stop the second big problem, soil erosion. In order to conserve soil and water by checking the run off, contour trenches and gully plugs were constructed along the hill slopes. Grass, shrubs and about 3 lakh (300,000) trees were planted along the hillside and the village. The villagers under Hazare's guidance also undertook fodder development, continuous contour trenches and loose boulder structures on 500 acres of land.

The watershed development work helped in conserving each drop of rainwater in the village itself and in recharging the groundwater aquifers. This ultimately raised the water table. In the same village where earlier it was not possible to cultivate more than 300–350 acres of land for one crop, now the villagers are harvesting two crops in 1500 acres of land. Due to availability of water, the agricultural production has boosted up. The agricultural development has created lot of employment in the village itself. Not only has the distress migration completely stopped, but now wage labourers have to be hired from other villages in order to get various intercultural operations done in time.

Ralegan has also experimented with drip and bi-valve irrigation in a big way. Papaya, lemon and chillies have been planted on a plot of 80 acres (320,000 m^2) entirely irrigated by the drip irrigation system. Cultivation of water-intensive crops like sugar cane was banned. Crops such as pulses, oilseeds and certain cash crops with low water requirements were grown. The farmers started growing high yield varieties of crop and the cropping pattern of the village also changed. He has helped farmers of more than 70 villages in drought-prone regions in the state of Maharashtra since 1975.

After the success of watershed development programme in Ralegan Siddhi, Hazare replicated it in the neighbouring four villages. The results are encouraging. Now the same project is being replicated in 80–85 villages of Maharashtra. The Government of India plans to start a training centre here to understand and implement Hazare's watershed development model in other villages in the country. On a visit to Ralegan Siddhi on 3 July 2010, Union Minister C.P. Joshi flanked by his department secretaries and other officials, tried to understand Hazare's style of watershed development, conservation and people power by creating strong rural leadership. Joshi said, "It is necessary to apply Anna's knowledge and experience to other villages. Despite many years of rural planning, many villages are still left out the government schemes. The success of Ralegan Siddhi can work wonders for others as well." State agriculture minister Balasaheb Thorat who was also present said, "The work in water conservation under Hazare's leadership is a model for the country."

Milk Production

As a secondary occupation, milk production was promoted in Ralegan Siddhi. Purchase of new cattle and improvement of the existing breed with the help of artificial insemination and timely guidance and assistance by the veterinary doctor has resulted in an improvement in the cattle stock. The milk production has also increased. Crossbred cows are replacing the local ones which give a low milk yield.

Earlier only 300 liters of milk was sold from the village. Now the milk production has gone up to 4000 liters. This milk is purchased by cooperative and private dairies. This brings in Rs. 1.3 to 1.5 crores (13 to 15 million) annually to the village. The dairy business has flourished as a subsidiary to agriculture which has provided a new income generation avenue to the unemployed youths of the village.

Some milk is also given to Balwadi (kindergarten) children & neighbouring village under the child nutrition program sponsored by the Zilla Parishad. From the surplus generated, the milk society bought a mini-truck and a thresher. Besides transporting milk to Ahmednagar, the mini-truck is also used for taking vegetables and other produce directly to the market, thus eliminating intermediate agents. The thresher is rented out to the farmers during the harvesting season.

Education

In 1932 Ralegan Siddhi got its first formal school, a single class room primary school. In 1962, the villagers added more classrooms through community volunteer efforts. By 1971 out of an estimated population of 1209, only 30.43 percent were literate (72 women and 290 men). Boys moved to the nearby towns of Shirur and Parner to pursue higher education, but due to socioeconomic conditions, girls could not do the same and were limited to primary education. Anna Hazare along with the youth of Ralegan siddhi worked to increase literacy rates and education levels. In 1976 they started a pre-school for the primary school and a high school in 1979. The villagers started taking active interest in the village school and formed the Sant Yadav Baba Shikshan Prasarak Mandal (Charitable trust), which was registered in 1979. The trust decided to take over the function of the village school which was in a bad state due to government neglect and also lack of interest on behalf of teachers who were moonlighting.

The trust obtained a government grant of Rs.4 lakhs for the school building using the National Rural Education Programme (NREP). A new school building was built in the next 2 months with volunteer efforts and the money obtained via the grant. A new hostel was also constructed to house 200 students from poorer sections of society. After the opening of the school in the village, a girl from Ralegan Siddhi became the first female in the village to complete her SSC in 1982. Since then the school has been instrumental in bringing in many of changes to the village. This school has a hostel for 150 boarders. Traditional farming practices are taught in this school in addition to the government curriculum.

According to the official website, the per capita income of the villagers has increased from Rs. 225 to Rs. 2500. This has completely transformed the economy of the village. The living conditions of the villagers have improved and the gap between the haves and have-nots has narrowed down. After the economic transformation of the village, villagers constructed buildings worth Rs.1 crore (10 million) for school, hostel and gymkhana and renovated the old village temple through financial contributions and shramdan.

Removal of Untouchability

Like any other village in India including Ralegan Siddhi, there was a social problem of untouchability. Today people of all castes and creeds live together in peace like members of the same family. The consecutive droughts led to non-payment of bank loans taken by the Dalit community for agriculture purposes. The bank decided to sell their mortgaged land to recover the loans. At this critical time, rest of the villagers decided to toil on the farmlands of Dalits and repay the loan by harvesting crops. The villagers cultivated their land in 1983-84 and 1984-85 through shramdan (voluntary labour), repaid the bank loan, and saved their land.

Collective Marriages

Most rural poor get into a debt-trap as they have to incur heavy expenses at the time of marriage of their son or daughter. It is an undesirable practice but has almost become a social obligation in India. Ralegan's people have started celebrating marriages collectively. The feast is held together where the expenses are further reduced by the Tarun Mandal taking the responsibility for cooking and serving the food. The vessels, the Loudspeaker system, the mandap and the decorations have also been bought by the Tarun Mandal members belonging to the oppressed castes. From 1976 to 1986, 424 marriages have been held under this system.

Gram Sabha

The Gram sabha is an important forum for collective decision making in the villages in India. If villagers are involved in the planning and decision making process, they are more open to any changes taking place in the village. Anna campaigned between 1998 and 2006 for amending the Gram Sabha Act, so that the people (meaning the villagers) have a say in the development works in their village. While the state government refused to bend to his demand, it had to give in due to public pressure. As per the amendments, seeking sanction of the gram sabha (collective of villagers, and not just the few elected representatives in the gram panchayat) for expenditure on development works in the village, is mandatory. In case of expenditure without the sanction of the gram sabha, 20 percent of gram sabha members can lodge a complaint to the chief executive officer of the zilla parishad with their signatures. The chief executive officer is required to visit the village and conduct an inquiry within 30 days and submit the report to the divisional commissioner, who has powers to remove the sarpanch or deputy sarpanch and dismiss the gram sevak involved. Anna was not satisfied, as the amended Act did not include "the right to recall a sarpanch". He insisted that this should be included and the state government relented.

In Ralegan Siddhi, the Gram Sabha meetings are held periodically to discuss issues relating to the welfare of the village. Projects like Watershed development activities are undertaken only after they are discussed in the Gram Sabha. All decisions like Nasbandi, Nasabandi (bans on alcohol), Kurhadbandi (bans on tree felling), Charai bandi (bans on grazing), and Shramdan were taken in the Gram Sabha. Decisions are taken in a simple majority consensus. In case of a difference of opinion the majority consensus becomes acceptable. The decision of the Gram Sabha is accepted as final.

In addition to panchayat, there are several registered societies that take care of various projects and activities of the village. In the last 35 years, many institutions and cooperatives like Gram Panchayat, Cooperative Consumer Society, Cooperative Credit Society, Cooperative Dairy, Educational Society, Women's Organisation and Youth Organisation, with different mandates are operating in Ralegan Siddhi. Till date no elections were held for the selection of members of these institutions. The members were selected unanimously by the villagers in the Gram Sabha. The Gram Sabha has emerged as a powerful forum for taking collective decisions at the village level. All the developmental programmes are implemented in the village after taking consent of the Gram Sabha.

Each society presents its annual report and statement of accounts in the Gram Sabha every year. The Sant Yadavbaba Shikshan Prasarak Mandali monitors the educational activities. The Vivid Karyakari Society gives assistance and provides guidance to farmers regarding fertilizers, seeds, organic farming, financial assistance, etc. Sri Sant Yadavbaba Doodh Utpadhak Sahakari Sansta gives guidance regarding the dairy business. Seven Co-operative irrigation societies provide water to the farmers from cooperative wells. Mahila Sarvage Utkarsh Mandal attends the welfare needs of the women.

Anti-corruption Protests in Maharashtra

Power Situation during 1985-86 became extremely critical. The farmers were unable to lift water from the wells in spite of its availability due to insufficient voltage to run pumps. The motors were getting burnt due to fluctuations and the crops were getting affected. There was scant response from the government in spite of continuous follow-up.

On 28 November 1989 Hazare was forced to undertake fast for seeking redressal. After 8 days of his fast, his health deteriorated and was admitted in the civil hospital at Ahmednagar. As there was, no response in spite of action from his side, the farmers from three tehsils became furious and they started road block agitation. Fearing that if the agitation takes a wrong turn, something untoward may take place, he appealed to the agitators from the hospital bed that they should not resort to unfair means, damage the national property and inflict any harm to the passengers. The agitation should be peaceful.

The police authorities did not expect huge participation and there was meager police force available. However, they were proved wrong and more than 10000 men and 1200 women participated in the agitation. The agitators had offered police to take them to jail. However, since enough transport was not available with the police, the police tried to remove the road block. Due to improper treatment meted out to the agitators, there was scuffle between police and the agitators and the police resorted to lathi-charged on agitators.

This action on the part of police irritated them and they pelted stones on the police force. Since the situation was going out of control, additional force was called and police opened fire on the agitators in which 4 farmers died on the spot and 7 farmers sustained severe injuries. Hazare felt sad on hearing this news in the hospital. The agitation was meant for awakening the government and there is no harm in carrying out such agitations in democracy. He had decided to end his life during the fast itself, but Senior Officials of the government and even Ministers persuaded him to give up his fast as they feared that if agitation continues, lot many farmers may lose their life and in order to save the life of innocent farmers, he withdrew his fast.

Adarsh Gaon Yojana

Model Village as contemplated by Gandhiji was brought in reality by Anna Hazare at Ralegan Siddhi by his dedication. "Late Shri Achyutrao Patwardhan, the great freedom fighter, suggested to the government of Maharashtra that to commemorate the golden jubilee of Bharat Chhodo Andolan, it would be most befitting to create model villages like Ralegan Siddhi in every tehsil of the state. The government accepted this suggestion and declared to implement "Adarsh Gaon Yojana". The Government entrusted this responsibility to him and Adarsha Gaon Yojana was started under his leadership. He travelled whole of Maharashtra and selected 300 villages to implement this scheme.

Anti-corruption Movements

In 1991, Hazare launched the Bhrashtachar Virodhi Jan Aandolan (BVJA) (People's Movement against Corruption), a popular movement to fight against corruption in Ralegan Siddhi. In the same year he protested against the collusion between 40 forest officials and the timber merchants. This protest resulted in the transfer and suspension of these officials.

In May 1997, Hazare protested against the alleged mal-practices in the purchase of powerlooms by the Vasantrao Naik Bhathya Vimukt Jamati Vikas Manch and the Mahatma Phule Magasvargiya Vikas Mandal. These institutions were directly under the charge of then Maharashtra Social Welfare minister Babanrao Gholap of the Shiv Sena, since their managing committees were dissolved after the Shiv Sena-BJP government came to power in the state in 1995. Hazare also raised the issue of alleged massive land purchase by Gholap's wife Shashikala in Nashik between April to September 1996. He forwarded the available documentary evidences in support of his allegations to then Maharashtra Governor P.C. Alexander.

On 4 November 1997, Gholap filed a defamation suit against Hazare for accusing him of corruption. He was initially arrested in April 1998 and was released on a personal bond of Rs 5,000. On 9 September 1998, Anna Hazare was imprisoned in the Yerawada Jail after being sentenced to simple imprisonment for three months by the Mumbai Metropolitan Court. The sentencing came as a huge shock at that time to all social activists. Leaders of all political parties except the BJP and the Shiv Sena came in support of him. Later due to public protests, the Government of Maharashtra ordered his release from the jail. After release, Hazare wrote a letter to then chief minister Manohar Joshi demanding Gholap's removal for his role in the alleged malpractices in the Awami Merchant Bank. Gholap resigned from the cabinet on 27 April 1999.

In 2003, the corruption charges were raised by Hazare against 4 ministers of the Congress-NCP government belonging to the NCP. He started his 'fast unto death' on 9 August 2003. He ended his fast on 17 August 2003 after then chief minister Sushil Kumar Shinde formed a one man commission, headed by the retired justice P.B. Sawant to probe his charges. The P.B. Sawant commission report submitted on 23 February 2005, indicted Suresh Jain, Nawab Malik and Padmasinh Patil. The report exonerated Vijaykumar Gavit. Suresh Jain and Nawab Malik resigned from the cabinet in March 2005.

Right to Information Movement

In the early 2000s, Anna Hazare led a movement in Maharashtra state, which forced the Government of Maharashtra to repeal the earlier weak act and pass a stronger Maharashtra Right to Information Act. This Act was later considered as the base document for the Right to Information Act 2005 (RTI), enacted by the Union Government.

Anna Hazare had to struggle for 11 years continuously against government for giving rights to citizens by making legislations for Right to Information, More Rights for the Gram Sabha, Regulating Transfers of the Government Officers, Prohibition and against Red Tapism.

- After the Shiv Sena—BJP government came in power on March 11, 1995; Anna Hazare started communicating with the government for taking steps to curb corruption. He wrote to the government 15 times and had meetings with it.
- He sent a letter to the government on January 12, 1998 asking it to make an act for Right to Information for checking corruption.
- As government was not paying any heed to his demand even after writing many letters and discussions, he started dharna on 6 April 1995 at the Azad Maidan, Mumbai.
- He again wrote to the government 10 times between April 6, 1998 and August 2, 1999 asking it to make the Act for Right to Information. In the mean time, Congress—NCP government came in power.
- He communicated with the newly formed government 5 times pressing it to make the Act. As it failed to do this, he wrote to the government on April 6, 2000 warning it that a statewide dharna agitation in front of Collector Offices would be started from 1st may and he would go on fast from 20th May, 2000.
- As per schedule, the dharna agitation started in front of all Collector Offices all over the state on 2nd May. The fast was postponed as the Central Government passed a bill in Lok Sabha on Information Technology.

- Continued communication with the government wrote 14 times and had meetings with the government one year lapsed.
- On 1st March 2001, wrote to the government that he would start statewide maun andolan from 1st May if the government did not make the legislation. The Chief Minister held a meeting with other concerned ministers and Secretaries and made a promise that the government will pass the bill in the coming session.
- After the promise from the Chief Minister, 81 days lapsed. Anna's correspondence with the government was continued. He wrote again on 1st March 2001 telling that he would undertake *maun* on 9th August 2001 at his native village Ralegan Siddhi.
- As per his warning, he started *maun* agitation on 9th August. On the same day, people started agitation all over Maharashtra.
- After 4 days of maun, the Minister of Law and Justice Mr. Vilas Kaka Undalkar visited Ralegan Siddhi to discuss with Anna Hazare. He facilitated a telephonic discussion with the Chief Minister and the Chief Secretary of Maharashtra. After promise from them, Anna stopped his maun.
- After the lapse of 1 year and a month and writing more than 15 letters, the government was not taking any action. So Anna started maun again on 21st September 2002. After 5 days, four Ministers of the Maharashtra Government, viz. Mr. Dilip Valse Patil, Shivajirao Kardile, Shivajirao Moghe and R.R. Patil came to Ralegan Siddhi for discussions with Anna Hazare. After getting a written assurance from the Chief Minister and Chief secretary, Anna stopped his agitation.
- A meeting between Anna Hazare and the government was

held on 30th October 2002 at Mumbai where the Chief Minister, the Chief secretary, other ministers and senior officers participated in the meeting on behalf of the government. Again a promise was made.

- But as the government was not keping its promise, Anna again warned on 21st January that he would undertake agitation on 20th February at Mumbai.

- In the men time, the Chief minister of Maharashtra got changed. The new CM Mr. Sushilkumar Shinde informed Anna Hazare that a solution would be found within a timeframe after a meeting with Ministers and Senior Officers. So Anna postponed his agitation.

- A high level meeting was held at the Secretariat in Mumbai on 17th February and the CM promised that appropriate action would be taken.

- After the failure of the government to keep its words, Anna again warned the government of agitation from 9 August 2003 at Mumbai.

- Anna finally went on fast on 9 August 2003 at the Azad Maidan in Mumbai. Thousands of people from all over Maharashtra gathered at the site of fast in support of his agitation. At the same time, people also protested at Collector Offices at all district headquarters. All this mounted tremendous pressure on the government. There was a threat of government collapse if the Act was not passed. Finally, the President of India signed the Bill on 12th day of Anna's fast and declared that the Act would be effective from 2002. Anna ended his fast at the hands of a noted Social Worker Mr. Tukaramdada Gitacharya.

- The Right to Information Act came into effect in Maharashtra from 2002. With Anna's persuasion, the same Act came into effect for the whole nation.

- Likewise, the Acts for more rights to the Gram Sabha and against Red Tapism were passed by the government.

In the Maharashtra State, a campaign was started demanding for the Right to Information. As Peoples Representatives and Civil Servants are public servants and the citizens of Maharashtra are owners of the public money, the citizens have the right to ask the public servants how and in what manner they spend the public money. He pressed for legislating an Act for Right to Information. The first campaign was organised at the Azad Maidan, Mumbai, in 1997. The State Government was giving only promises, but it failed to crystallize it in many sessions of the Vidhan Sabha. He had to make agitations, *dharnas, morchas, maun* and fasts many times.

State-wide tours were held for awareness generation among people. Public addresses were organised in many towns and programmes were arranged specially for college students. Posters, banners and folders were printed and distributed in thousands. All this resulted in the awakening of the citizens and making them aware of their fundamental Right to Information.

The Government made many promises, but it failed to keep one. Any government never wants to decentralize its power and hand over power to people. Many politicians think that decentralisation of power will lessen their importance, status and respect. So the Government was reluctant to make legislation for Right to Information.

Finally, with zeal of 'do-or-die', Hazare went on fast-unto-death on August 9, 2003 at Azad Maidan, Mumbai. He decided that unless the Act is passed by the Government, he will not end his fast; rather he will sacrifice his life for people's rights. The Government of Maharashtra felt that his resolution is firm and He would not step back from his decision of 'do-or-die'. On the

12th day of his fast, the Government of Maharashtra got the Bill signed by the President of India and enacted the law of 'Right to Information' in Maharashtra. The Act on 'Right to Information' is a revolutionary step towards strengthening democracy.

Due to this Act, transparency has come in the administration. Now a common man can get information by just paying a nominal charge of Rs. 10 or 20. This has paved the way to good governance and healthy democracy.

If this Act reaches every village and every household, it has potential to check corruption to an extent of 80-85 percent. Due to corruption, only 10 percent could reach the real beneficiaries of the poverty alleviation programmes earlier. Rest of the money percolated to the purses of corrupt officers and politicians. Now, due to the Act of Right to Information, the poor villagers will get their due share in the development process. The quality of project works has started to improve after the Act.

Central Government Stopped Amendments in Right to Information Act

It is a positive step after 58 years of Independence to enact the Right to Information Act. But as this Act has potential to check corruption to a great extent, some politicians felt it as a hurdle in their corrupt practices. Prime Minister Manmohan Singh's Government tabled a Bill for amendments in the existing Act which were detrimental to the very cause of the Act. Citizens had got these rights after 58 years of Independence after a long struggle. The proposed amendments were going to nullify these rights. To protest against the amendments, Hazare undertook fast unto death at Alandi near Pune.

Within two days of commencing his fast, people in various parts of Maharashtra started agitation on their own in support of his demand. People undertook '*Rail-roko-andolan*' (train blockade) at nine places. Gradually, the agitation spread to other parts of India. Even some Indians residing in the US went on fast in support of my agitation. Prime Minister Manmohan Singh sent one of his Ministers as emissary to Alandi, as the agitation gathered momentum in and outside the country, and promised that the existing Right to Information Act would not be amended by the Central Government. He requested Hazare to end his fast and he gave it up on 9th day. Fortunately, the Government gave up the idea of proposed amendments in the Right to Information Act.

Act for Regulating Transfers

As there was no clear-cut policy on transfers of the Government Officers, the People's Representatives and Senior Officers of the government misused their power to transfer the government servants as per their wish. In these transfers, usually money changes hands. Thus, a transfer was a source of bribery.

If an elected Representative wants his relative or confident to be posted in a key position where an honest Officer is already working, he would misuse his power to get the honest man transferred to other place; thus creating vacancy to bring his man to that position. This was injustice to the honest officer.

To prevent this type of injustice, he started a movement for legislation of an Act which would prevent transfer of any officer, at the will of his superiors or political heavy weights, for a minimum period of three years. It was also ensured that no officer will continue at the same place for more than three years. The local politicians like Members of the Lok Sabha and Vidhan Sabha, Ministers in the Government and Senior Officers of the Government opposed legislation of this Act as it was going to affect their vested interest. Due to this Act, the honest officers got some relief and the corruption involved in transfers has reduced to a large extent.

More Rights for Gram Sabha

Gram Sabha is a Village Parliament; just like Lok Sabha and Vidhan Sabha being parliaments at Central and State levels respectively, in the Indian parliamentary system of democracy. Gram Sabha is supreme in the democratic set-up. Any villager who attains the age of 18 years automatically becomes a member of the Gram Sabha according to provisions in the Indian Constitution. Villagers, who are eligible for casting their votes by virtue of their age, are the members of the Gram Sabha. There is no election for constituting the Gram Sabha as in the case of Lok Sabha or Vidhan Sabha. It is an autonomous and sovereign body. The members of the Gram Sabha elect the members of the Lok Sabha and Vidhan Sabha through elections who subsequently form the Lok Sabha and Vidhan Sabha. Thus, the Gram Sabha is the mother of Lok Sabha and Vidhan Sabha. The Ministry of the Government, may it be at Central or State level, has to take the Lok Sabha or Vidhan Sabha into confidence for undertaking any developmental programme. In the same way, the Gram Panchayat, i.e. the elected body at village level, should take the Gram Sabha into confidence before undertaking developmental programmes.

A peoples movement was carried out for 7 years for legislation for granting more rights to Gram Sabha. Finally, the State Govt. of Maharashtra passed an Act granting more rights to Gram Sabha. Now, it is made mandatory for the Gram Panchayat to take permission of the Gram Sabha before spending the money it receives from the government for different developmental programmes. If it is found that the Gram Panchayat did not take permission of the Gram Sabha and spent the money without information to the Gram Sabha, then the villagers (minimum 20 percent of voters) could approach the Chief Executive Officer (CEO) of the Zilla Parishad for an enquiry into the expenditure. The CEO has to make an enquiry within a month and, if he is convinced that the money has been spent without the knowledge of the Gram Sabha, send his report to the Divisional Commissioner recommending for legal action. There is provision in the Act that the Divisional Commissioner can dismiss the Sarpanch (Head of the Gram Panchayat), the Deputy Sarpanch and the Gram Sevak (Village Development Officer).

The Act has helped in bringing transparency in village development schemes and thus curbing corruption to a great extent. Every citizen has a right to elect his representative in the democracy. In the same way, he should also have a right to recall the elected representative. This Act has given this right to recall to the villagers. This will foster a healthy and people-oriented democracy. There is a need for awareness generation and educating people to use this Act for bringing more transparency in the development programmes.

Anna's Personal Clarification

Anna Hazare is simple man and his life philosophy is also very simple. But his achievements are not so simple. Although his life's works speaks so loud, those don't need any clarification, but he always clarifies. His achievements have won him many awards like the Indira Priyadarshini Vrikshamitra award, the Krishi Bhushana award, the Padma Shree, Padma Bhushan and the Ramon Magsaysay award. Care International of the USA, Transparency International, Seoul (South Korea) also felicitated him.

Here is the brief clarification about himself collected form his different media-bites:

For me there is no black-and-white. It's either black. Or white. My tirade against corruption has taken me places-into the hearts of thousands of Maharashtrians (people from the Indian state if Maharashtra) and others all over the country!

I feel that when even Alexander the Great could not carry anything with him on his journey to heaven, then why this craving for the materialistic? What's life after all? To be good to others. In fact, *seva mein hi anand hai* (to serve is to be happy). This message took root in me in the mid-60s. And continues to inspire me. I'm not going to give up. And I am ready to sacrifice all for the sake of my commitment. My life is for my countrymen. The fight for corruption is my agenda. I have clear goals. And a well chalked-out plan for fighting corruption.

The subject of corruption has often seen me lock horns with political bigwigs. But irrespective of that, I want more changes to take place. Change in the education system will automatically help a child to grow in a healthy atmosphere. With schools and colleges accepting bribes in the form of donations, what do you expect of a child? What path will they follow? The Official Secrets Act is a weapon overused in India. Anything the government wishes to hide is pushed under the carpet. I want this Act to be abolished. The right to information is a fundamental right of every citizen. But it remains only on paper. Why? We need a certain time-frame for access to information. I am all for more powers at the village level.

Clearly, the corridors of power breed corruption. And Delhi, India's capital, comes high on the list. It will take time to mobilize people to fight corruption, but yes, we are working towards it. T.N. Seshan, former Indian Chief Election Commissioner, took it up in a big way, but then lost control midway. His brush with politics has sullied his earlier grand image. Time and again, I have also been approached by Indian political parties including the BJP, Shiv Sena and Congress to join them. But I am adamant. My mind was made up against joining politics long ago. It's a trying situation though. People with a clean image should enter politics.

I am, at times, accused of being publicity-hungry. Believe me, if I were like that, I would only get pain in life. I follow the Gita's teachings. And fully understand that short-term gains don't get you anywhere. I am also accused of being caste-conscious. This is unfair. I know I feel for certain issues from the bottom of my heart. People often ask me why corruption is talked about so much these days. I feel there's a limit to everything. People have tolerated enough and have run out of patience. Survival for the common man is difficult.

I wonder why people do not understand that in a republic, power is meant to be vested in them. But power has gone to politicians or bureaucrats although they are considered public servants. How ironic! So, what do we do with the enemy within? I think we need another round of the freedom struggle. And people involved in it should be ready to go to jail and give up their lives, as they did in the effort to throw out the British.

For me this is rebirth. During the 1965 war against Pakistan I was in the Army. All my colleagues died in Khemkaran. I survived. Later, at New Delhi railway station I picked up a book by Swami Vivekananda. It changed my outlook towards life. A decade later I took voluntary retirement. And ever since it has been a struggle...

References

Websites

http://www.annahazare.org/
http://indiaagainstcorruption.org

Other Sources

1. "Padma Bhushan Awardees". Retrieved 10 April 2011.
2. "India activist Anna Hazare ends hunger strike". *BBC News*. 9 April 2011. Retrieved 9 April 2011.
3. "Government issues notification on committee to draft Lokpal Bill". New Delhi: *The Hindu*, 9 April 2011. Retrieved 9 April 2011.
4. "Anna Hazare: The man who can't be ignored". *The Times of India*. 7 April 2011.
5. Ghosh, Avijit (17 April 2011). "I was re-born in the battlefield of Khem Karan". *The Times of India*. Retrieved 17 April 2011.
6. "From driver to driving force". *The Hindu*. 8 April 2011. Retrieved 11 April 2011.
7. Gosling, David L. (2001). tBYHXrQfLhaGJAw&sa= X&oi=book_result&ct=result&resnum=3&ved=0 CEUQ6AEwAg#v=onepage&q=Anna%20Hazare%20 Pakistan%20war&f=false *Religion and ecology in India and*

Southeast Asia. London: Routledge. pp. 64–6. ISBN 0-415-24031-X.

8. Seabrook, Jeremy. *Victims of Development: Resistance and Alternatives.* London: Verso. pp. 109-17. ISBN 0-86091-385-6.

9. Raghuvanshi, C.S. (1995). *Management and Organisation of Irrigation System.* New Delhi: Atlantic. p. 44. ISBN 81-7156-560-3.

10. *Springs of life: India's water resources.* Academic Foundation. 2006. pp. 392. ISBN 817188489X, 9788171884896. Retrieved 8 April 2011.

11. Deshmukh, Vinita (7 April 2011). "Anna Hazare, our one, big hope, and why he can do it". Moneylife. Retrieved 8 April 2011.

12. Sharma, Reeta (20 January 2001). "Anna Hazare: A fearless crusader". *The Tribune.* Retrieved 9 April 2011.

13. Sharma, Kalpana (8 April 2011). "Anna Hazare: India's pioneering social activist". Mumbai: BBC. Retrieved 9 April 2011.

14. "Hazare hails govt move to ban gutkha". Mumbai: *Indian Express.* 9 July 1997. Retrieved 9 April 2011.

15. "Activist fights Indian Corruption". Ralegan Siddhi: Southeast Missourian. 1 December 1996. Retrieved 7 April 2011.

16. "Govt to set up training centre at Ralegan Siddhi". Pune: *Times of India.* 3 July 2010. Retrieved 8 April 2011.

17. Deshmukh, Vinita (12 September 2004). "The Village Roadshow". *The Indian Express.* Retrieved 8 April 2011.

18. "Anna Hazare visits KISS". Bhubaneswar: *The Hindu.* 18 Aug 2010. Retrieved 8 April 2011.

19. Marothia, Dinesh K. (2002). *Institutionalizing Common Pool Resources.* New Delhi: Concept Publishing. pp. 122-8. ISBN 81-7022-981-2.

20. "The rise and rise of Anna Hazare". *India Today*. 6 April 2011. Retrieved 9 April 2011.

21. Raman, Anuradha; Smruti Koppikar (18 April 2011). "Wielding The Broom". *Outlook*.

22. "Hazare trains guns on Gholap". *Indian Express*. 21 May 1997. Retrieved 8 April 2011.

23. "Hazare released on bond in Gholap case". *Indian Express*. 14 April 1998. Retrieved 8 April 2011.

24. "Anna Hazare sentenced to three months imprisonment". *Indian Express*. 10 September 1998. Retrieved 8 April 2011.

25. "Anna Hazare's arrest". *Anna Hazare's arrest*.

26. "Hazare sentenced". *Anna Hazare sentenced*.

27. "Hazare wants Gholap sacked". *Indian Express*. 12 December 1998. Retrieved 8 April 2011.

28. Marpakwar, Prafulla (28 April 1999). "Snap polls woke Rane up to sack Gholap". *Indian Express*. Retrieved 10 April 2011.

29. "Pawar-Hazare rivalry revived". *The Statesman*. 6 April 2011. Retrieved 8 April 2011.

30. "Anna Hazare ends protest fast". Rediff.com. 17 August 2003. Retrieved 8 April 2011.

31. Bavadam, Lyla (12 March 2005). "A probe report and politics".*Frontline* Volume 22, Issue 07. Retrieved 8 April 2011.

32. "Sawant Commission submits report". Rediff.com. 24 February 2005. Retrieved 8 April 2011.

33. Damle, Manjiri Madhav (29 June 2004). "Trust funds used for Hazare's birthday: Jain". *The Times of India*. Retrieved 17 April 2011.

34. "Nawab Malik is second NCP minister to quit". *The Times of India*. 11 March 2005. Retrieved 8 April 2011.

35. Florini, Ann. *The Right to Know: Transparency for an Open World*. New York: Columbia University Press. p. 24. ISBN 978-0-231-14158-1.

36. Roberts, Alasdair. *Blacked Out: Government Secrecy in the Information Age*. Cambridge University Press. p. 3.ISBN 9780521858700.

37. "Anna Hazare calls off fast on RTI amendment". *The Times of India*. 19 August 2006. Retrieved 11 April 2011.

38. Deshpande, Vinaya (29 March 2011). "Anna Hazare faults Lokpal Bill". *The Hindu*. Retrieved 5 April 2011.

39. "Anna Hazare to start fast unto death for strong Lokpal Bill". *Hindustan Times*. 5 April 2011. Retrieved 5 April 2011.

40. "India activist Anna Hazare anti-graft fast stokes anger". BBC. 7 April 2011. Retrieved 7 April 2011.

41. "Thousands join Anna Hazare's anti-graft fight". 6 April 2011. Retrieved 6 April 2011.

42. "Uma Bharti, Chautala heckled at Hazare protest". 6 April 2011. Retrieved 9 April 2011.

43. "Support pours in for Hazare's movement".

44. "Bollywood supports Anna Hazare". *nowrunning*. 6 April 2011. Retrieved 6 April 2011.

45. "Sharad Pawar quits corruption panel as support for Anna Hazare grows".

46. Anna Hazare Fight Against Corruption Has Taken A Social Media Turn. Digitalanalog.in (7 April 2011). Retrieved on 7 April 2011.

47. "Northeast support to Hazare's". GUWAHATI/ SHILLONG/ AIZAWL: Times of India. 9 April 2011. Retrieved 9 April 2011.

48. "Government issues notification to constitute a joint drafting committee to prepare draft Lok Pal Bill". New

Delhi: Press Information Bureau, Government of India. 8 April 2011. pp. 1. Retrieved 9 April 2011.

49. "Lokpal Bill: Text of Gazette notification". New Delhi: The Hindu. 9 April 2011. Retrieved 9 April 2011.

50. Lakshmi, Rama (9 Apr 2011). "India agrees to protesters' demand on graft panel". *The Washington Post* (Bangalore). Retrieved 9 April 2011.

51. "Anna Hazare ends fast, says his fight against corruption to continue". New Delhi: *India Today.* 9 April 2011. Retrieved 9 April 2011.

52. "India wins again, Anna Hazare calls off fast". New Delhi: *Times of India.* 9 Apr 2011. Retrieved 9 April 2011.

53. "Anna Hazare wins Rabindranath Tagore peace award". New Delhi: Daily India. Apr 8, 2011. Retrieved 12 April 2011.

54. Pandharipandhe, Shyam (16 April 2008). "Anna Hazare— the keeper of the earth and human conscience". Pune: *RxPG news.* Retrieved 9 April 2011.

Index